Tolley's
Managing Violence in the Workplace

Tolley's
Managing Violence in the Workplace

Bill Fox, Charles Polkey and Peter Boatman
of Maybo Limited

Tolley
LexisNexis™

Members of the LexisNexis Group worldwide

United Kingdom	LexisNexis Butterworths Tolley, a Division of Reed Elsevier (UK) Ltd, 2 Addiscombe Road, CROYDON CR9 5AF
Argentina	LexisNexis Argentina, BUENOS AIRES
Australia	LexisNexis Butterworths, CHATSWOOD, New South Austria
Austria	LexisNexis Verlag ARD Orac GmbH & Co KG, VIENNA
Canada	LexisNexis Butterworths, MARKHAM, Ontario
Chile	LexisNexis Chile Ltda, SANTIAGO DE CHILE
Czech Republic	Nakladatelství Orac sro, PRAGUE
France	Editions du Juris-Classeur SA, PARIS
Hong Kong	LexisNexis Butterworths, HONG KONG
Hungary	HVG-Orac, BUDAPEST
India	LexisNexis Butterworths, NEW DELHI
Ireland	Butterworths (Ireland) Ltd, DUBLIN
Italy	Giuffrè Editore, MILAN
Malaysia	Malayan Law Journal Sdn Bhd, KUALA LUMPUR
New Zealand	Butterworths of New Zealand, WELLINGTON
Poland	Wydawnictwo Prawnicze LexisNexis, WARSAW
Singapore	LexisNexis Butterworths, SINGAPORE
South Africa	Butterworths SA, DURBAN
Switzerland	Stämpfli Verlag AG, BERNE
USA	LexisNexis, DAYTON, Ohio

A CIP Catalogue record for this book is available from the British Library.

ISBN 0 7545 1967 8

Typeset by Columns Design Ltd, Reading, England
Printed and bound in Great Britain by Antony Rowe Ltd, Chippenham, Wilts

Visit Butterworths LexisNexis *direct* at www.butterworths.com

Contents

List of Diagrams

About the Authors

Charles Polkey, Bill Fox and Peter Boatman are specialists within the leading conflict management firm Maybo Limited. The authors draw on first-hand experience in dealing with challenging behaviour and violence, and each is a respected authority in management strategy and training in this field. In this handbook the authors share learning from their pioneering work with a diverse range of organisations and sectors.

The authors would like to thank Sheila Hawkins and the Employment NTO for their support with writing CHAPTER 3. They would also like to acknowledge Michael Appleby, Dr Anthony Bleetman, Jim O'Dwyer, Simon Imbert, and John Davison for their guidance. Thanks also goes to Sally, Jane and Stephanie for their patience and understanding. The authors also wish to mention their Maybo colleagues who helped with the development and testing of the key models and approaches contained within the handbook, and in particular the transformational work of Nick Strapp and David Currie. Finally, the authors would like to thank the organisations that have provided the real life case studies, and the committed managers and staff who have shared their experiences.

Foreword

It is a sad but inescapable fact that criminal violence in society has been increasing. Equally disturbing, is the fact that violence in the workplace is keeping up with this trend. In the latter case there is however a difference in the sense that employers and managers can formulate policies and procedures and training programmes to ensure that the risk to their employees from members of the public, and the risk to those in the care of their employees, is minimised. Over the last few years much publicity has (quite rightly) been focussed on assaults on nurses and staff in accident and emergency departments by drug addicts, drunks and others, and sometimes by mentally disturbed patients. By the same token publicity has focussed on violence or the threat of it by public service workers against those in their care. Although not so luridly captured by the media, notice has been drawn to restaurant workers and other service providers in the private sector that are also subjected to violence by those they are endeavouring to serve. This not only includes nightclubs, shops, hotels and public house employees, but also the leisure industry and public transport premises and vehicles.

This handbook is not written for the academic, although it will be of interest to those with a theoretical as opposed to a practical interest in the subject. It should be a must for the employer, trade union or staff association representative, as well as the individual who experiences both the threat and the manifestation of violence in their work. The authors of this handbook possess practical experience in identifying the likely areas where problems are most likely to occur. They have also shared their knowledge in extensive training programmes aimed at averting violence, or when that is not possible, minimising its effect. The handbook covers existing legislation and sanctions that are available to the innocent victim. The number of case studies and examples of best practice alone give an insight into the authors' depth of knowledge and worthiness of their professional advice based on their practical experience. The handbook provides useful discussion on workplace violence, which so many employers have to their discredit, unfortunately, just hoped wouldn't happen in their back yard. However, as the case studies and reported workplace assaults each year illustrate, if you are not prepared, then it will happen.

Employers and managers have a duty of care to their employees and to those members of the public, whether patients, students, passengers, or other users of the services provided by that organisation. This handbook explains in straightforward terms the legislative framework in an area that might otherwise be viewed as complex and complicated. The law may not be simple but this handbook deals with it in an easy to understand format leaving no doubts as to both the rights and the obligations of employers, managers and workers alike.

Work-related violence does happen and every year millions of people are affected directly or indirectly by it. No employers' or staff associations' bookshelves can be complete without this handbook and access to it's content is both sensible and essential for workers and supervisors alike, particularly for those in the caring professions such as nurses, teachers and other service providers who cannot choose their customers or clients. I firmly believe that we all have a duty to ensure that health and safety in the workplace, which includes the reduction or elimination of work-related violence, is a top priority in what should be a civilised society.

Lord Imbert of New Romney, QPM JP
Former Commissioner of the Metropolitan Police (1987–1993)
Chairman of Capital Eye Security Ltd and
Capital Eye Policing Support Services Ltd

1 Introduction

Introduction and context

1.1   The health and safety of people at work has been a matter of concern in the United Kingdom for many years and a great deal of practice, procedure and legislation has been developed to minimise the tangible risks of coming to harm in the workplace environment. The hazards of machinery, construction work, chemicals and dangerous substances are all too obvious and the need for appropriate measures for minimising such risks is unquestionable.

In contrast, violence in the workplace has only recently been taken seriously across the wide range of sectors where the risks are not immediately apparent. The likelihood of violence being inflicted upon a police officer or security guard is fairly obvious, but it has taken some time for the alarming realisation that our nurses, doctors, teachers and social workers are increasingly facing the risk of serious violence whilst trying to carry our their roles.

Workers in most sectors can relate to incidents of violence and the overwhelming belief is that the problem is getting worse. This handbook focuses on violence directed towards employees from those they come into contact with. This can include patients, customers, clients and passengers, depending on the nature of the organisation. Within the text the term 'service user' will sometimes be used to embrace all the variations. The term violence includes verbal abuse, threats, intimidation and physical assault.

Internal conflict between employees such as harassment and bullying is an equally serious issue, but needs to be dealt with in its own right as a separate matter as strategies for managing it are different.

Numerous explanations are offered for the increase in violence towards workers including:

- Higher expectations of service users leading to conflict.
- Willingness of individuals to complain and demand what they want.
- Smoking bans and their enforcement.
- Increased stress associated with complex modern life.
- Steady increase in violent crime.
- Changing values and beliefs surrounding acceptable behaviour.

- Popularisation of violence through television and media.

- Negative role models such as football and rock stars – ie does this make violence appear to be acceptable?

Alcohol remains one of the most common factors contributing to violence.

The prevention and management of violence is often more complicated than managers first realise, as there can be many complex causes of the problem and many factors that influence its successful control. Success is usually achieved through a holistic approach that starts with assessing and reducing risk, and considers how we respond to incidents and their effects. This handbook follows these stages and seeks to provide practical support to those managers and practitioners tackling this growing problem.

The nature and extent of the problem

1.2   Other than *RIDDOR (SI 1995/3163)*, the ways in which organisations report, record and analyse incidents of workplace violence are diverse and unique to each one. Indeed, some organisations record very limited information, which provides virtually no insight into the problem at all. Most organisations and studies acknowledge that even where reporting mechanisms exist, incidents are grossly under-reported. As a consequence, there is very little empirical data in the United Kingdom from which we can gain a broad picture of the extent of the problem. Fortunately, the British Crime Survey (BCS) has been collecting data about workplace violence for several years.

The BCS provides a count of crime across England and Wales and includes crimes not reported to or recorded by the police. From 1986 it was conducted bi-annually but since 2000 is now conducted on a yearly basis.

The definition of workplace violence used in the survey is:

'All assaults or threats which occurred while the victim was working and were perpetrated by a member of the public'.

In 1999 the Health and Safety Executive (HSE) commissioned the Home Office to carry out a retrospective analysis of data from the BCS, relating to violence at work covering the period from 1991 to 1997. The report, Tracey Budd 'Violence at work: New findings from the 2000 British Crime Survey' (July 2001) London Home Office, estimated that there were over 1.2 million incidents of violence at work in 1997. The number of incidents increased significantly between 1991 and 1995, but then fell by 19% between 1995 and 1997. Even so, the number of incidents in 1997 was still above the number reported in 1991.

The 2000 BCS showed a 5% increase to the number of violent incidents during 1999 bringing the figure up to 1.3 million. Although this does not firmly establish a trend, it does suggest that the 19% fall between 1995 and 1997 may well have been reversed.

Who is at risk?

1.3   The 2000 BCS provided a detailed breakdown contained in the following table which combined the 1994, 1996 and 1998 data to show the occupations which carried an above average risk of assault or threat of assault from members of the public.

Occupation	*High risk of assaults* Average risk = 1.2%	*High risk of threats* Average risk = 1.5%
Security and protective services	11.4%	5.3%
Nurses	5.0%	3.1%
Public transport	2.8%	5.6%
Catering/hotels/restaurants	2.6%	2.0%
Other education and welfare	2.6%	2.3%
Teachers	1.8%	2.0%
Retail sales	1.8%	3.5%
Management and personnel	1.7%	2.6%
Leisure/service providers	1.7%	1.9%
Other health professionals	1.4%	4.0%
Care workers	2.8%	–
Cashiers, bank managers, and money lenders	–	2.0%

Notes:
1. Source: Combined 1994, 1996 and 1998 sweeps of the BCS. Weighted data.
2. Measures risks of violence at work in 1993, 1995 and 1997.

Table 1.1: Occupations with above average risks of violence while working, 1994/1996/1998 British Crime Survey (based on working adults of working age)

The survey found that almost half of the number of assaults at work and a third of threats at work happened after 6 pm. Given that for most people, the working day does not extend past 6 pm these results demonstrate that the risks of violence are higher for those working during the late evening or night.

A sixth (16%) of physical assaults at work involved offenders under the age of 16. Young offenders were less often mentioned in threats (8%). Most incidents involving young people were against teachers and other education and welfare workers, though many were against those in the security and protective services.

The report also looked at the extent to which workers were worried about being assaulted or threatened at work. The survey found that 17% of workers who had some form of contact with members of the public were worried about being assaulted. Unsurprisingly, those in occupations with a higher risk of violence, such as public transport workers, nurses and teachers, were most concerned.

To put all this in perspective, although the total number of reported incidents seems to be high, the estimated risk of an employee being assaulted or threatened in a given year is actually relatively low. The BCS estimated that 2.5% of working adults had been the victim of at least one violent incident at work in 1999; 1.2% had been physically assaulted and 1.4% had been threatened. This is, of course, cold comfort to the actual people who represent those statistics.

In 1999 the Trades Union Congress (TUC) published 'Violent Times' a key report on preventing and managing violence at work. Among its findings the TUC highlighted that one in five workers are subject to a violent attack or abuse at work every year. Nurses were identified as being the group most at risk with one in three being attacked, followed by those working in the security industry. Care workers and education and welfare employees were also highlighted as higher risk groups. The report stated that the vast majority of security guards had no training in dealing with aggressive members of the public, even though they were often employed to protect other workers and property.

The cost of work-related violence

1.4   The impact of work-related violence is difficult to quantify and once again there is very little empirical data in the UK that helps to clarify this.

The cost can be viewed in three different ways:

1.   The impact upon the individual employees in terms of their health and confidence to perform their role effectively.

2.   The cost to employers in terms of lost working time.

3.   The impact on customers, clients, patients and service users.

For the reasons already discussed, we rely once again on the BCS for some insight into the impact of workplace violence. In the 2000 study, just under half of the assaults at work resulted in an injury of some sort and in almost 1 in 10 of the incidents, the victim saw a doctor as a result of the incident. Three quarters of victims reported that they had been emotionally affected by the incident. The most common reactions were shock, anger and fear.

The 1998 survey estimated that 3.3 million hours were lost due to work-related violence in 1997 and the compensation that victims believed they were entitled to amounted to £180 million.

More than half of the victims said they needed some form of help after the incident and a third of victims said they had sought or received help from their employer.

The BCS noted that just over half (55%) of assaults and a third (37%) of threats were reported to the police. This reinforces the chronic under-reporting of incidents of work-related violence, especially threats, which is endemic in most organisations. It suggests that there may be many incidents which come within the definition of violence at work that people do not report because they feel it is not worth it or that they just have to put up with it because 'it goes with the job'.

The focus should be to look beyond the statistics. Although an assault on a colleague in some workplaces may be rare, it will still have a considerable impact on individuals and organisations. The fear of violence will significantly effect performance because personal safety is a basic human need. If people are fearful that that they are working in an unsafe environment then they will be distracted by that fear and their motivation to provide a good service will be suppressed. If, on the other hand, that fear is removed then they will be able to concentrate upon the service they are providing. This shows a strong 'business case' for tackling this issue, in addition to the moral and legal requirements.

Drivers for change

1.5   Recent years have seen a change in the attitude towards issues of work-related violence. The UK Government is driving a climate of 'zero tolerance' towards violence generally, and in the workplace in particular, encouraging organisations to develop robust responses to the problem. Several areas, notably the health, public transport and education sectors, have responded with high profile campaigns aimed at reducing the risks. Trade unions and professional bodies have also responded with research, advice and guidance aimed at preventing incidents and helping victims.

The HSE publishes general and sector-specific guidance to help employers to prevent and manage the risk of violence towards staff. In March 2000, the Health and Safety Commission embarked on a three-year partnership programme to achieve a 10% reduction in work-related violence by the end of the programme, using the 2000 BCS figures as a benchmark.

An effective campaign against violence will raise awareness of the problem and the need to report incidents. The HSE recognises that this is likely to lead to an increase in reported incidents in the short term. This has in fact been the experience of the NHS Executive in its high profile initiative against violence with the zero tolerance campaign which set a target of a 20% reduction of violence in 2001, yet saw a 30% increase in reporting of incidents.

In the 2000 BCS, 18% of workers said that they had received formal training in their current job about how to deal with violent or threatening behaviour; 72% had not received any formal training or informal advice. Even amongst the high-risk groups the level of training provision did not exceed 50%, with the exception of security and protective services where 71% received training. These are worrying figures – a major part of any drive for change must be the investment in training and development of staff who are at risk.

The introduction of the new National Occupational Standards in Managing Work-related Violence will, for the first time, provide an integrated and standardised approach to the whole issue of work-related violence across all sectors. This will lead to a greater sharing of best practice and a better understanding of the nature of the problem both nationally and at a sector-specific level. A better understanding will, in turn, lead to the introduction of more effective measures to combat the problems. They also leave employers in no doubt about the standards that are expected of them in this area.

Organisations which represent the interests of employees, in particular trade unions and professional associations, have been providing a lead in this area for some time. They are building up an important information bank which will inform both employers and employees of the risks of violence faced across the different sectors together with practical advice and guidance about appropriate measures which will reduce the risks.

For the few employers who are unmoved by other drivers, the increasing litigation that is being instigated in relation to workplace violence should be of concern. Employees are much more ready to seek compensation and redress for injuries and stress-related illnesses resulting from work-related aggression and violence and there are plenty of avenues for them to do so.

National Occupational Standards in Managing Work-related Violence

1.6   CHAPTER 3 provides a unique insight into the new National Occupational Standards in Managing Work-related Violence by Sheila Hawkins, who led this project whilst working with the Employment National Training Organisation. The Standards take a comprehensive overview of each key element of strategy in managing work-related violence.

How to use this handbook

1.7   This handbook has been written specifically with the practitioner in mind. It is intended to provide a useful and practical guide to:

- Developing and implementing an effective policy for dealing with workplace violence.

- Risk assessment in relation to work-related violence.

- Measures for reducing conflict and risk of violence.

- Providing targeted and appropriate training and development.

- Relevant legislation including the use of force.

- The management of incidents – including post-incident issues.

Key points

1.8   Each chapter covers a main topic area and key points are listed to summarise the main issues.

Checklists

1.9   Checklists are offered as a practical tool to help implement some of the guidance in the handbook. Each checklist provides a framework for ensuring that all practical concerns, issues and tasks required are addressed when, for example, designing a policy for workplace violence in an organisation.

Case studies

1.10   The advice and guidance offered in this handbook is illustrated by a number of case studies of organisations that represent the issues and problems faced across the main sectors. They have been chosen because each has made significant progress in one or more of the key areas featured in the handbook. This is not to suggest they have a perfect solution – such solutions rarely exist – and some of the organisations featured are still in the early stages of their response. However, all can claim to have made progress towards creating a safer workplace, and their approaches provide food for thought.

Throughout the book the case studies will show how the practicalities of introducing new policies, training programmes, working practices etc were tackled and overcome. CHAPTER 7 TRAINING uses case studies extensively to highlight the range of approaches an organisation can take and key success factors.

The case studies

1.11

- **Ambulance Partnership Against Violence Project**

  Six ambulance trusts, UNISON, and conflict specialists, Maybo, worked in partnership to identify the specific training needs of ambulance personnel. The London Ambulance Service has a dedicated Staff Safety Officer addressing violence towards staff and along with the Welsh Ambulance Services, West Yorkshire Metropolitan, Tees East and North Yorkshire, and Royal Berkshire Trusts, is delivering highly tailored training to staff. The West Yorkshire Trust is also doing pioneering work in the area of post-incident management.

  Focus of case study:

  o   Undertaking a Training Needs Analysis.

- **Hamish Allan Centre, Glasgow City Council**

  The Hamish Allan Centre is concerned with the provision of accommodation and support services to the homeless, and has developed a multi-faceted strategy to reduce the likelihood and impact of conflict and violence.

  Focus of case study:

  o   Policy – undertaking a comprehensive management review of the problem.

  o   Training – key considerations in training design.

- **British Institute of Innkeeping (BII)**

  The British Institute of Innkeeping is the professional body for the licensed retail sector. As part of its remit the Institute operates the National Certificate For Door Supervisors – Licensed Premises, which contains specific training on conflict management and physical interventions.

  Focus of case study:

  o   Approaching physical intervention training.

- **North West London Hospitals NHS Trust**

  This large NHS Trust incorporates the Central Middlesex and Northwick Park hospitals. As in other Trusts, violence towards staff is real concern.

Focus of case study:

o   Responding to the diverse support and training needs within a large Trust.

- **Institute of Conflict Management (ICM)**

The ICM has set out to raise standards in the field of conflict management and provide a conduit for members to exchange information regarding best practice. The Institute has played a key role in the development of the new National Occupational Standards in Managing Work-related Violence.

Focus of case study:

o   Raising standards.

- **London Borough of Havering**

This large London borough has a number of directorates, each with very different training needs. The Council has managed to provide a consistent core of training in managing aggression and violence whilst tailoring this to meet the different needs of each directorate and work group.

Focus of case study:

o   Training implementation strategy.

- **London Borough of Croydon – Parking Services**

Parking Services staff in various roles face abuse on a regular basis. Managers recognised the importance of delivering high quality training to staff and also in evaluating the effectiveness of this training in the workplace.

Focus of case study:

o   Workplace evaluation of training.

- **Servisair**

Airport ground handling specialist Servisair has developed conflict-management training for its staff at the customer interface, in areas such as check-in and airside. Servisair has developed its own internal capacity to deliver this 'Managing the Tough Stuff' training.

Focus of case study:

o   Internal trainer development.

- **Select Service Partner (SSP)**

Select Service Partner (SSP) (the travel market subsidiary of Compass Group plc) recognises that its employees can at times come across difficult people when working at its UK network of rail station bars and retail outlets. Although the programme is still in its early stages, SSP has developed an innovative approach to the potentially daunting task of training large numbers of staff spread out across the UK.

Focus of case study:

o   Combining internal and external capability in terms of strategy, training, incident reporting and staff support.

- **Nando's**

Nando's operates a chain of family restaurants based mainly in inner city areas. The company trains its restaurant managers on how to be proactive in creating a safe and welcoming environment for staff and customers.

Focus of case study:

o   Manager development and staff support.

- **South West Trains Ltd**

South West Trains Ltd has made a substantial commitment to training managers and staff with a view to improving personal safety and customer service. The company has also introduced Travel Safe Officers as another thread in its strategy to create a safer environment for staff and customers.

Focus of case study:

o   Training strategy and Travel Safe Initiative.

- **Virgin Trains**

Virgin Trains are committed to delivering personal safety training to customer facing staff across the whole company and are integrating this with the roll out of new trains. They recognised the need to develop their internal training team in the skills necessary to facilitate scenario-based learning.

Focus of case study:

o   Internal/ external training partnership.

- **Hastings Borough Council**

Hastings Borough Council has invested in personal safety training across the organisation using an external consultant. It was concerned about selecting appropriate people to form a new team of street wardens and used the consultants to assist in this process.

Focus of case study:

o   External consultants – recruitment of new staff through assessment centres.

- **Brighton Buses**

Brighton Buses is providing training for drivers in how to deal with conflict and risk situations, and has also introduced a response team trained to assist drivers that come into difficulty whilst on the road.

Focus of case study:

o   Staff and response team training.

- **Northamptonshire Police**

Northamptonshire Police has been at the forefront of police 'officer safety' with former Officer Safety Co-ordinator Inspector, Peter Boatman, receiving the Queens Police Medal for his personal contribution. The organisation has developed a comprehensive, dedicated violence reporting and monitoring process, and has also undertaken extensive research on the issues of protective vests and safer restraint devices.

Focus of case study:

o   Reporting, monitoring and risk reduction.

2 Work-related Violence – the Legislation

Introduction

2.1   This chapter outlines the framework of legislation that is used in the United Kingdom to deal with the issues of work-related violence. In general, the framework is the same as for any other health and safety issue and therefore it is summarised in the context of workplace violence. The emphasis is on providing a practical and workable understanding of the law – rather than a detailed academic understanding.

The focus is upon the law relating to the type of incidents where the violence is committed against an employee by someone who is a service user or someone not connected with the organisation. Whilst not wishing to detract from their seriousness, the issues of bullying and harassment by one employee against another are not within the remit of this handbook.

The chapter ends with a brief review of the law relating to self-defence and the use of force – an important area that is often misunderstood. This will help managers and trainers to understand employees' rights and powers, and to take these into consideration when writing a health and safety policy and guidance notes – thus avoiding the development of policies that place unreasonable and sometimes unlawful restrictions on an employee's response in an extremely violent situation. The guidance is also useful for developing content for training programmes.

In Northern Ireland the law largely mirrors that of England and Wales. Scots law has more obvious differences, some of which are covered in this handbook. It is important that readers seek specific advice as to the applicability in their particular legal jurisdiction.

The framework of UK legislation

2.2   In common with most countries, in the UK there is little new legislation or regulation designed to deal specifically with the issues of work-related violence. Instead, we need to look to several existing laws that provide for regulation, enforcement and remedy in such cases.

In simple terms, the law provides:

*   Regulation to ensure that employers provide a working environment in which the risks of being subjected to violence are

minimised and the fears of employees are taken into account. Employees also owe a duty of care to themselves and to others who may be affected by their acts or omissions.

- Enforcement to provide sanctions if employers fail to comply with the regulation and punishment of individuals who act violently towards another person in a workplace context.

- Remedy for employees who become victims of workplace violence. This will usually be in the form of compensation through an industrial tribunal, civil court, or criminal injuries compensation board.

Figure 2.1: Framework of legislation

The main sources of legislation in relation to workplace violence are:

- **Health and safety legislation**

  The legislation relating to the general principles and requirements that exist for health and safety at work are utilised to embrace workplace violence amongst all the other hazards that manifest themselves in the working environment. The reporting requirements of the *Reporting of Injuries, Diseases and Dangerous Occurrences Regulations 1995 (RIDDOR) (SI 1995/3163)* also apply to cases of work-related violence.

- **Employment law**

  Two aspects of employment law are particularly relevant on the issue of violence. Both contract law and the *Employment Rights Act 1996* have relevance to the responsibilities of both employer and employee in this context. A contract of employment brings with it mutual obligations and the employer has a clear obligation to provide a safe working environment, which includes safety from violence. The *Employment Rights Act, s 44* further addresses the rights and responsibilities of the employer and the employee and makes an important contribution on the issue of withdrawal of service.

- **Criminal law**

  The criminal law relating to public disorder, assault, threats and harassment is available as a means for prosecuting offenders in appropriate circumstances eg where an affray or assault has occurred.

- **Civil law**

  There are a number of ways in which a victim of workplace violence can claim compensation through the civil courts. For example, compensation can be sought against the employer for negligence where there has been a 'breach of duty'. There could also be a civil court claim against the individual for 'assault'. The *Protection from Harassment Act 1997* can also be used to pursue a civil remedy as well as for prosecuting where a criminal offence is committed.

The impact of each of the above in the context of work-related violence will now be examined.

The statutory requirements under health and safety law

2.3   There are five main pieces of health and safety law, which are relevant to violence at work.

Health and Safety at Work etc Act 1974

2.4   Employers have a legal duty under the *Health and Safety at Work etc Act 1974 (HSWA 1974)* to ensure, so far as is reasonably practicable, the health, safety and welfare at work of their employees. [*HSWA 1974, s 2(1)*].

Besides a common law 'duty of care' to others, employers have a statutory duty to do 'everything reasonable and practicable' to 'eradicate or minimise' the risk of harm from all hazards to health – including violence.

Employers are also required to conduct their undertaking in such a way as to ensure, so far as reasonably practicable, the safety of other people who are not their employees, and to whom the premises have been made available.

The 1974 Act is considered as the most important piece of legislation dealing with health and safety at work. Although it was implemented to cater for the risks associated with industries such as chemicals, mining and construction work, the basic principles are translated relatively easily within the context of the protection required against the risks of workplace violence. Lord Skelmersdale, who chaired the DHSS Advisory Committee on Violence to Staff, wrote in the 1988 report:

> 'Where violent incidents are foreseeable employers have a duty under section 2 [of the Health and Safety at Work etc Act 1974] to identify the nature and the extent of the risk and to devise measures which provide a safe workplace and a safe system of work.'

Health and safety legislation has moved away from prescriptive laws that stipulate how things should be done, to goal-setting laws that direct what needs to be achieved. The basis of the goals is risk assessment.

The important words in *section 2* of the *HSWA 1974* are 'so far as is reasonably practicable' (often referred to as 'SFAIRP'). The test as to what is reasonably practicable was set out in the case of *Edwards v National Coal Board [1949] 1 All ER 743*. This case established that the risk must be balanced against the 'sacrifice', whether in money, time or trouble, needed to avert or mitigate the risk. By carrying out this exercise the employer can determine what measures are reasonable to take. This is effectively an implied requirement for a risk assessment.

The Health and Safety Executive publication, 'Successful Health and Safety Management', HSG 65, says that accidents and ill health are seldom random events. They generally arise from the failure of control and involve multiple contributory causes.

The duty of care also embraces employees. Employees are required under *section 7* of the *HSWA 1974 to* 'take reasonable care for the health and safety of himself and of other persons who may be affected by his acts or omissions at work'. The duties placed on the employee do not reduce the responsibility of the employer to comply with his health and safety duties under the 1974 Act.

Management of Health and Safety at Work Regulations 1999

2.5 The *Management of Health and Safety at Work Regulations 1999 (MHSWR) (SI 1999/3242)* require employers to consider the risks to employees. The risks covered should, where appropriate, include the need to protect employees from exposure to reasonably foreseeable violence. Employers must:

- Establish how significant these risks are.

- Identify what can be done to prevent or control the risks.

- Produce a clear management plan to achieve this.

In summary this places obligations on employers to ensure that employees are:

- Advised in easily comprehensible terms about the risks they face.

- Suitably qualified to carry out the role.

- Properly supervised.

- Trained to a standard that is 'commensurate with the level of risk being faced'.

- Guided against practices known to be unsafe.

- Informed of the procedures for dealing with 'serious and imminent danger', and for entering danger areas.

- Authorised, and under no apprehension about stopping work and withdrawing from, circumstances which make it unsafe to do otherwise, and prevented from resuming work whilst a 'serious and imminent' danger exists.

- Monitored for signs and symptoms that they may be suffering harm eg stress.

Workplace risk assessment is well established within environments where dangerous machinery, substances and conditions exist. Measures taken as a result will include the use of protective clothing and equipment, adopting safer work procedures and practices and appropriate training. Where there is a risk of violence to employees while undertaking their work, then risk assessments and control measures are equally appropriate and measures will include training in dealing with aggression and violence, and the creation of safer working environments and working practices. These control measures will be looked at in more detail in **CHAPTER 6** and training is covered specifically in **CHAPTER 7**.

To achieve the requirements under the Regulations, employers must put into place a comprehensive policy for dealing with work-related violence. This will include effective measures for identifying and assessing risk, clear guidelines and procedures for dealing with violent incidents and their aftermath, and the provision of appropriate training and equipment.

It is worth noting some forthcoming amendments to health and safety legislation:

- Breach of the *HSWA 1974* and the *MHSWR (SI 1999/242)* do not give rise to civil liability. However the Health and Safety Commission has proposed that the *MHSWR* be amended to remove the civil liability exclusion.

- There are proposals to amend the *MHSWR* to require *RIDDOR* matters to be investigated and linked into risk assessment.

Reporting of Injuries, Diseases and Dangerous Occurrences Regulations 1995

2.6   Employers must notify their enforcing authority in the event of an accident at work to any employee resulting in death, major injury or incapacity for normal work for three or more days. This includes any act of non-consensual physical violence done to a person at work. [*Reporting of Injuries, Diseases and Dangerous Occurrences Regulations 1995 (RIDDOR) (SI 1995/3163)*].

Many reporting systems are geared around the *RIDDOR* requirements. However, to gain a comprehensive and useful database of information about patterns and trends in workplace violence, the reporting system should cover a great deal more than the basic requirements of *RIDDOR*.

Safety Representatives and Safety Committees Regulations 1977 and the Health and Safety (Consultation with Employees) Regulations 1996

2.7   Employers must inform and consult with employees in good time on matters relating to their health and safety. Employee representatives either:

- appointed by recognised trade unions under the *Safety Representatives and Safety Committees Regulations 1977 (SI 1977/500)*; or

- elected under the *Health and Safety (Consultation with Employees) Regulations 1996 (SI 1996/1513)*,

may make representations to their employer on matters affecting the health and safety of those they represent.

This places a responsibility on the employer to consult and inform on issues of violence at work. This is becoming more frequent and some organisations now have comprehensive guidelines for their employees who are at risk from workplace violence. It has to be said that a large number of organisations have little or no policies, working practices or appropriate training to deal with work-related violence.

Employment law

Employment Rights Act 1996

2.8   *Section 44* of the *Employment Rights Act 1996 (ERA 1996)* relates to 'Health and safety cases' and reminds us that responsibility for safety at work is something shared between employers and employees. The section covers:

- Employees statutory entitlement to a safe way of working, and to be able to fulfil their responsibility under the *HSWA 1974, s 7* to take care of themselves and others, without fear of recriminations ('any detriment') from their employer for doing so.

- The circumstances in which an employee should withdraw from danger (covered later under 'Withdrawing services' in **2.13**).

- Employees duty and right to be able to draw attention to safety deficiencies that may exist and to take 'appropriate action' to withdraw/ remove themselves from 'serious and imminent' danger that they would be unable to avert.

- Warning to employees that if they continue to knowingly and recklessly undertake work that is unsafe and get injured they may not be able to make a claim against their employer for liability.

Contract law

2.9   A contract of employment imposes two obligations on the part of the employer.

- The employer must provide a workplace in which employees are subjected to minimal exposure to risk.

- The employer must provide 'trust and support' to the employee in carrying out their role.

These obligations exist whether or not they are explicit in the contract and regardless of the organisation or the type of work being undertaken. It is well established that workplace violence should be regarded as a risk in this context. The employer is expected to provide 'trust and support' to ensure that the employee is working under minimum stress and that the employer responds to issues of perceived risk as well as real risk. This is illustrated by the well-established case of *Keys v Shoe Fayre Ltd [1978] IRLR 476* where an employee was required to take money to the bank. The employee was worried about being mugged when carrying out this duty and there had been some instances of mugging in the area. The person refused to take money to the bank and was subsequently sacked because of it. It was held that the employer had failed in his obligation of trust and support because he did not take his employee's concerns seriously or explore alternative ways of getting money to the bank. This was therefore considered to be a breach of contract.

Failure to provide appropriate support might reach a point where an individual can no longer tolerate the working conditions and decides to leave. This could be construed as constructive dismissal where the situation is treated as if the employee had been dismissed. The individual will usually seek a remedy through an industrial tribunal or a county court.

The obligations of an employer are unambiguous. There is a clear requirement to assess the possible risk of an employee being subjected to violence and to provide appropriate measure which will minimise that risk. There is also a requirement to recognise and respond to the perceived fears of employees by providing appropriate support in relation to those fears.

Criminal law

2.10   The laws in relation to violence, disorder, assault and threats are well established and cover almost every incident of work-related violence. Thankfully, the incidence of serious assault is comparatively rare but this brings with it a difficulty in relation to prosecuting the offender. In general, it requires the police to pursue the matter to prosecute the offender and many different issues have to be addressed when making the decision.

Quite often the nature of the assault is not serious enough for a criminal charge to be pursued or, for a variety of reasons, the circumstances do not warrant it. It is unlikely that an assault that results in only minor bruising, for example, would find its way into a court. Whilst these decisions often make economic, procedural or legal sense, they leave the victims feeling frustrated and unsupported. A common cause of dissatisfaction felt by employees who have been assaulted is related to the apparent lack of action that follows the incident. They expect the offender to appear in court to answer for his or her conduct, only to find that the police have cautioned him or her or the Crown Prosecution Service has declined to take the case further. Victims are not impressed by the economic, legal and evidential arguments that are put forward to justify the decision. For the victim, even though there was no serious assault, the incident was often very frightening, very public and left them in a good deal of shock and distress. They are often left feeling 'let down by the system'.

In such cases, the reasons for the decision needs to be communicated fully to the employee and any alternative action that can be taken should be discussed. Organisations also need to be careful about the promises they make; some 'zero tolerance' type initiatives sound good on paper and posters but may not be able to deliver in practice and succeed only in raising expectations that cannot be met.

A number of benefits can come from liaising with local police managers to discuss their response to incidents and their views on prosecution. The police and local authority community safety representatives will also be able to advise on some aspects of risk reduction and local initiatives.

If the police do not charge an assailant the employer can support the individual through either a private criminal prosecution or a civil prosecution. Such action will send important messages to both employees and service users.

It is also important to recognise the important role that documentation takes in any legal case, and particularly in a criminal case. Generally, all written documents associated with the incident are disclosable – that is copies must be given to the defence prior to the court case. For this reason, the accuracy and consistency of documents like notebooks, work diaries, statements, incident and accident report forms, is of vital importance. Seemingly watertight cases can be undermined by the exposure in court of inconsistencies and inaccuracies that seemed of little consequence at the time they were made.

Among the range of powers now available for dealing with violence and the fear of violence is the *Protection from Harassment Act 1997*. The Act is often associated with 'stalking' but has much wider use in dealing with anti-social conduct. A person must not pursue a course of conduct which amounts to harassment of another *and* which he knows or ought to know amounts to harassment of the other.

Harassment is not strictly defined but often includes some alarm, distress or torment that has some adverse impact on the victim. This conduct can include speech and does not necessarily have to constitute violence. The test will be if a reasonable person would believe the conduct to be harassment. The conduct needs to have taken place on at least two separate occasions for an offence to be complete, and the police have a power of arrest. Damages can be sought and injunctions can be applied for. Convicted persons can also have restraining orders placed upon them, for example, against contacting the victim(s).

Many offences carry extra penalties if proven to be racially aggravated, and these will be recorded by the police as crimes and can constitute a more serious offence under the *Crime and Disorder Act 1998*. The 1998 Act also introduced anti-social behaviour orders, which provide another option for dealing with ongoing problems within a community.

In the second part of this chapter certain aspects of criminal and common law will be looked at in more detail.

Negligence

2.11 In cases where the victim has suffered serious injury, either mental or physical, they will undoubtedly look for substantial compensation for things like their loss of earnings, pain, suffering, and inconvenience. Although it is clear that the person who actually committed the act of violence is directly at fault, it is unlikely that the individual will have the funds to provide for any substantial compensation award. Consequently, the victim will be more likely to seek redress through his or her employer by claiming that the employer was negligent in providing appropriate measures to prevent the incident from happening, and/ or in failing to provide adequate support post-incident (leading to further stress and 'psychiatric injury').

In such cases, key questions will be asked:

- Was violence in the workplace something that ought to have been assessed?

- If so, what were the risks of violence that would have been identified in the risk assessment?

- What reasonably practicable control measures would the risk assessment have identified should it have been put in place?

As to the meaning of risk, in *R v The Board of Trustees of the Science Museum [1993] 3 All ER 853* the Court of Appeal said that risk means the possibility of danger and not actual danger. However note the words of Hale LJ in *Koonjul v Thameslink Healthcare Services [2000] PIQR P123*, CA, in which she says there has to be a *real risk* and not just a *mere possibility of danger* and went on to say:

' ... there must be a real risk, a foreseeable possibility of injury; certainly nothing approaching a probability ... '

There has been an increasing amount of publicity in recent years about the issues of violence in the workplace and it features as a topic in the media on at least a monthly basis. It is debated regularly in trade and professional publications, and is a focus within the Government, local authorities and trade unions. In short, it is unlikely that an employer would succeed in a claim that he was unaware of the issue. The obligations of risk assessment under health and safety legislation also mean that employers in many areas of work would have difficulty in arguing that they did not reasonably foresee a risk. The 'reasonable steps' will depend upon particular circumstance, but it would be reasonable to provide training, safety equipment and advice on working practices and procedures.

Many of the major legal actions have focussed on stress resulting from both single acts of violence, and that which has taken place over an extended period. The resulting claims against the employer may be based more on the lack of support and care following the incident. Post-incident management and employee support is examined in depth in CHAPTER 9.

Employers must also be realistic about the demands placed on staff in their work and to take this into consideration in selection and training. A 1999 case that highlights this was that of Beverley Lancaster who won significant compensation from her local authority employer as a result of the stress that followed a forced change in role. The switch from a clerical job to a customer-facing role in a neighbourhood housing office involved exposure to conflict involving disgruntled tenants. The authority apparently did not train Mrs Lancaster for her new role and failed to recognise her plight. This case was significant in its recognition that stress could lead to mental injury and – as with physical injury – that this risk can and must be assessed and preventative action taken.

The 'payouts' surrounding an employer's breach of duty of care can be very high, particularly where this results in stress-related illness. This is highlighted by the settlement of just over £200,000 to a county council warden in 2000. The warden left his job as a result of stress from ongoing verbal and physical abuse whilst working on travellers' sites, and an apparent lack of appropriate management support.

A Court of Appeal ruling in February 2002 in the case of *Sutherland v Hatton [2002] ECWA Civ 76*, laid down important guidelines in respect of injury claims arising from work-related stress. Much of the guidance revolves around whether this kind of harm to a particular employee was reasonably foreseeable. The duty to take reasonable steps is triggered by impending harm to health, which must be plain enough for any reasonable employer to realise it has to act.

There is a breach of duty only if the employer has failed to take steps that are reasonable in the circumstances, bearing in mind the magnitude of the risk of harm occurring, the gravity of that harm, the costs and practicality of preventing it and the justifications for running the risk.

In all cases it is necessary to identify the steps that the employer could and should have taken before deciding whether there has been a breach of duty of care. Breach of duty does not have to be the only cause of the psychiatric injury in order for the claimant to succeed in getting compensation. However it does have to be, what lawyers call, a 'material contribution'

For example, the employer may successfully argue he could not have prevented an attack on an employee, which is seen as being the cause of the psychiatric illness suffered by the employee. However failure to provide adequate aftercare may be a material contribution. This argument comes from the case of *McGhee v National Coal Board [1973] 1 WLR 1*. This was a dermatitis case. The claimant succeeded on the basis that the defendant had not provided adequate washing facilities. The court found that this materially increased the risk of the claimant getting dermatitis and so was a material contribution.

The provision of a confidential advice service, with appropriate counselling or treatment services is a key step in supporting employees and in protecting the organisation against criticism.

Vicarious liability

2.12   In recent years the boundaries have been extended even further for a company's responsibility for its employees' actions. Vicarious liability is the legal concept whereby a company can be held liable for the negligent conduct of its employees. A claim for compensation for personal injury will be successful if the conduct occurred during the course of employment.

In a fairly recent Court of Appeal ruling a train operating company was held vicariously liable for the violent actions of an employee towards a person on a station platform. Even though the employee had acted way beyond the parameters of the job role, the incident occurred while he was on duty and the employer was vicariously liable for his actions.

A recent case (below) illustrates how wide the concept can be applied.

In *Lister v Hesley Hall [2001] 2 All ER 769* the claimant attended a boarding school for maladjusted and vulnerable boys. He was sexually abused by a warden at the school, who was later convicted. The claimant brought a claim for compensation against the school arguing the conduct occurred during the course of employment. The House of Lords agreed and compensation was awarded.

This case shows employers can be liable for an employee's criminal as well as negligent conduct and that vicarious liability can apply even though the employee is acting outside instructions.

Withdrawing services

2.13   At what point is it appropriate for an employee to say that they are not prepared to continue because they feel they are in danger? This is a question which is faced from time to time where an employee feels that they are in danger of being physically hurt and they are not prepared to continue to deal with a situation. The employer needs to have a contingency built into the policy for this eventuality and have clear guidelines. It is not sufficient to leave the guidelines so broad as to be meaningless but equally it is near impossible to cater for every foreseeable circumstance.

Legislation provides help in this area.

Section 7 of the *HSWA 1974* requires employees to take reasonable care for the health and safety of themselves and others. This implies that the employee has the right to withdraw their service if it is required to protect themself or others from harm.

Regulation 8(1)(a) of the *MHSWR 1999 (SI 1999/3242)* states that 'Every employer shall —establish and where necessary give effect to appropriate procedures to be followed in the event of serious and imminent danger to persons at work in his undertaking'. *Regulation 8(2)(b)* of the 1999 Regulations enables the persons concerned to stop work, and immediately proceed to a place of safety in the event of their being exposed to serious imminent and unavoidable danger.

Section 44(1)(d) of the *ERA 1996* prescribes the circumstances when an employee should withdraw their service as:

> 'in circumstances of danger which the employee reasonably believed to be serious and imminent and which the employee could not reasonably have been expected to avert ... '

The law fully protects employees against suffering any detriment as a consequence of adopting this course of action – as long as the action was taken in the employee's reasonable belief that the risk was serious and imminent and that he or she could not prevent it happening. Whether the steps that an employee took were appropriate will be judged by reference to all the circumstances including, in particular, the employees knowledge and the facilities and advice available to them at the time.

Section 44(3) of the *ERA 1996* makes it quite clear that if an employee acts negligently and then suffers detriment as a consequence they will not be able to make a claim for liability against their employer. Actions will be judged against what an ordinary cautious person might have done.

Clearly, it is not sufficient for a policy to say 'walk away at the first sign of trouble'. Most roles that encompass direct contact with the public inevitably involve dealing with a certain level of frustrated and angry people and such an approach would be completely unworkable. Indeed, the enforcement nature of some roles is such that frustrated and angry people may be regarded as an inevitable part of the job. Enforcement duties often draw employees into situations where they fail to withdraw from a threatening situation because they become driven by their perception of their role. If a member of the public for instance refuses to pay, or to produce a ticket, or allow an inspection of their premises etc, it is easy to be drawn into blocking someone's exit, engaging in an argument or detaining the person concerned. Employers must provide very clear guidelines as to the action the employee is expected to take – and actions he or she must not engage in – in such circumstances and at what point they must withdraw from their duty. This must be underpinned by training – if the employee is expected to detain they need to understand the law in relation to detaining a person and practice the appropriate physical intervention skills to enable them to do it lawfully and safely. If they need to withdraw, they need to know how to achieve it safely and, wherever possible, without losing face.

The increasing number of call centres has highlighted the issue of abusive callers on the telephone. Many call centres provide excellent, clear guidelines about abusive calls and the process to follow if a caller becomes particularly abusive with precise information about how to terminate a call if it becomes necessary to do so.

Dangerous or unpleasant

2.14   It is important to make a distinction between situations that are dangerous and those where the task is unpleasant. Many roles have some tasks and duties that are more unpleasant than others. Paired working provides a good example, which although a valid risk reduction measure in some instances, can sometimes be seen as a simple solution and an automatic right. However, the expectation of the employees for paired working could be based more on having a colleague to share the workload and to provide company, than on an actual increase in risk during that time. Although it is important to recognise the legitimate fears and perceptions of staff, it is also important that the decision is based upon some objective view of the risks. The result may be that paired working is established for certain tasks, times or places, and not as a matter of course. Paired working doesn't necessarily prevent employees being assaulted, and the perceived increase in confidence could even result in greater risk taking and potential for conflict. It is important that training focuses on how to maximise safety when working with a colleague and operate effectively as a team.

Impact for the employer

2.15   The legislation clearly imposes upon an employer the same level of responsibility that exists for providing a safe working environment in other aspects of health and safety. There is a case for recommending that workplace violence should be tackled as a separate issue to ensure that the it does not become 'lost' in the general health and safety responsibilities. Organisations should undertake a specific review and assessment of risk in relation to workplace violence for every role.

Any organisation that is at risk of work-related violence is vulnerable unless it devises and implements a specific violence at work policy. This should include an effective system for recording and analysing incidents and for identifying and providing appropriate training, safer procedures, and protective equipment.

These measures should recognise the need to respond to employees' perceptions and fears as well as 'hard facts' and reality. Employers should also recognise the need to provide for effective after care. Victims are often left feeling distressed, shocked and traumatised and may need considerable support for their return to normal duties.

Key points

- There is very little legislation in the United Kingdom that is specifically aimed at dealing with work-related violence.

- Criminal law however provides offences and punishment for incidents of violence, disorder, assault and threats.

- There is a framework of legislation drawn from different sources that provides regulation, enforcement and remedy for incidents of violence.

- Regulation and enforcement of the risks of workplace violence are provided for within the existing general regulatory framework in relation to health and safety at work. Sector-specific legislation (eg *Education Act 1996*) is beginning to emerge as awareness of the issue increases.

- Employment law sets out rights and duties on both the employer and the employee on health and safety matters, and contract law provides remedies, often through industrial tribunals, where the employment contract is not fulfilled.

- The law of negligence is often used by victims to claim substantial compensation for serious injuries sustained.

- Employers need to assess the risk of violence and put in place policy and control measures that reduce its incidence and impact on staff, in order to fulfil obligations to employees and reduce vulnerability to litigation.

- Stress resulting from conflict and violence at work can result in psychiatric injury and – as with physical injury – this risk can and must be assessed and preventative action taken.

- The provision of a confidential advice service, with appropriate counselling or treatment services is a key step in supporting employees and in protecting the organisation against criticism.

The law relating to the use of force and self-defence

2.16 The law relating to self-defence is reasonably clear and unambiguous. However, society has a curious attitude towards 'defending oneself and one's property', which probably has its origins in the playground ie 'if I hit you, you can hit me back'. This is reinforced by a surprising number of parents who, when their son arrives home with a black eye, send him off to find the culprit and do the same to him. As a consequence, confusion develops about the legitimacy of retaliation as opposed to self-defence. This has been highlighted recently by the case of the Norfolk farmer who shot a young man dead whilst he was climbing out of the window of his house; and the Deputy Prime Minister, John Prescott, who punched a man who had thrown an egg at him. It is not intended that the rights and wrongs of these cases are debated here, merely to point out the sizeable lobby, in both cases, who supported the rights of the individual to retaliate – rather than merely defend.

This confusion extends to the workplace where employees who are faced with angry and violent customers take retaliatory action – rather than action that can be regarded as self-defence. 'If someone spits at me, I couldn't help but punch him!' is a classic response often heard in training sessions. Although being spat upon is a disgusting act, it would be very difficult to defend a resulting punch in terms of self-defence.

Organisations where staff are clearly exposed to a risk of assault are often wary of encouraging staff to take physical action towards a customer, client or other individual who is becoming aggressive. This is understandable, and often results in the introduction of 'no touch' or 'walk away' policies. These are commendable from the point of view that they are introduced to stop staff getting hurt. However, such policies are often unworkable in practice, particularly when staff find themselves in situations where they have to defend themselves. The policy might well have the opposite effect – they get hurt because they are afraid to take the appropriate action which will break the organisation's guidelines. Staff need a realistic policy – together with a firm understanding of the actions they can take – and the responsibilities and consequences that might flow from those actions.

The following section outlines the law in relation to self-defence and the use of force in work-related situations.

In law any use of force is an assault and is unlawful unless justified. The offence of assault can actually be complete without any physical contact. If someone is being physically threatened and he or she believes the other person can carry out that threat then the other person is committing an assault. In strict terms the law refers to assault and battery. Assault is effectively the fear of being attacked. Being hit constitutes a battery.

There are of course exceptions to this liability provided for in law, making it lawful in certain circumstances for one person to assault another.

Common law powers to use force – self-defence

2.17

'Any person may use such force as is reasonable in the circumstances in defence of themselves or others and in certain circumstances, property'.

It is therefore recognised at common law that there are occasions and circumstances where a person may use force on another without committing an offence.

At common law force can therefore be used to:

- Prevent or ward off unlawful force (assault).

- Rescue another person from attack or prevent an attack.

- To avoid or escape unlawful detention.

In such circumstances the force used must be reasonable in the circumstances and no more than is necessary to repel any attack. It is also accepted that a person does not have to wait to be attacked before they can act to defend themselves, although some attempt should be made to retreat where practicable.

The term 'reasonable' is not defined as it is recognised every set of circumstances will be different. The seriousness of the situation will be taken into consideration and the options that were available to those involved. The individual's perception of the situation will also be taken into account and their honestly held belief that they or others were in imminent danger. An extreme example being the case where police officers have shot a person in possession of a toy gun. The courts also recognise that in the heat of the moment it is difficult to measure the use of force 'on a jewellers scale', and will need to be sure that a person had only done what he/ she honestly and instinctively thought necessary when defending themselves against unlawful attack.

It is important that the terms reasonable and necessary are explored during training and put into context by looking at the likely scenarios staff face in their role. More recently, this now has to be viewed in the context of the *Human Rights Act 1998*, which is dealt with in **2.22**.

Common law powers to use force – trespass

2.18   At common law people admitted to private premises are there at the 'licence' of the owner or occupier of those premises. That licence can be refused so people may not enter, or if people are admitted the licence can be withdrawn and the person becomes a trespasser. People therefore have a right to refuse entry to premises, or require people to leave their premises. This power can extend to managers and those employed as security guards or door supervisors. In the case of those who do not own or occupy the premises they can be said to be acting as a servant or agent of the owner. With that authority such persons can refuse entry, or withdraw the licence and require people to leave.

As well as people having the power to use force for protection there also exists the power to use force to prevent unauthorised entry (trespass), or to eject a person who has entered as a trespasser, or who has become a trespasser due to their licence to be on the premises being withdrawn.

The same rules governing the use of force being reasonable and necessary still apply. Where a person is required to leave there is also the need to allow them a reasonable opportunity to do so before force is used. It is wise in most instances to call the police before attempting to physically remove a trespasser.

Common law powers to use force – saving a life

2.19   At common law this power to use force to protect a life also includes action to save a life. This could apply in a situation where an individual is attempting suicide or is about to put the lives of others at risk.

This is not always straightforward as hospital trusts have found when for example, staff within an accident and emergency department prevent a patient from leaving and treat them against their will. This situation raises concerns over assault and human rights issues, yet by not acting to protect the person, the hospital could also be criticised for failing in their duty of care.

A key consideration in this example is the capacity of the patient to understand and retain information about the treatment they need, the consequences of not receiving it, and their ability to make a proper, balanced decision on this basis.

This capacity may be diminished for a number of reasons including mental health problems, medical condition, alcohol or drug use, and sometimes the effect of the treatment itself.

Other common law powers

2.20   There is a common law right to protect property and also a common law power to prevent a 'breach of the peace'. Any person can arrest a person who:

- has committed a breach of the peace;

- is committing a breach of the peace;

- is about to commit a breach of the peace and there are reasonable grounds to suspect this.

This covers harm to a person or (in his presence) harm to his property.

This aspect of the law is rarely covered in training as many managers fear it may be abused.

Statute law

Criminal Law Act 1967, section 3

2.21   The key piece of legislation in relation to use of force is *section 3* of the *Criminal Law Act 1967*. Whilst other statutes give specific powers to police and other agencies, *section 3(1)* of the 1967 Act also gives rights to any person to use force as follows:

'A person may use such force as is reasonable in the circumstances in the prevention of crime, or in effecting or assisting in the lawful arrest of offenders or suspected offences or persons unlawfully at large.'

Anyone using force in such circumstances is personally responsible and may be required to justify their actions in court. Where police officers use force relying on this section they are in exactly the same position and cannot simply rely on their status as police officers or any orders given to them as a means of defending against either criminal or civil litigation. The same requirement (as in common law) for this force to be reasonable and necessary applies.

The use of the words 'lawful arrest' is important. If the arrest of that person is not lawful then no use of force in effecting the arrest can be lawful and the person effecting the arrest may be liable to both civil and criminal proceedings. It is important that staff who are likely to be involved with the arrest of persons committing crime, such as security officers and store detectives, have a clear understanding of relevant sections of the *Police and Criminal Evidence Act 1984 (PACE)*, and in particular the powers of arrest. This Act details powers and procedures that need to be followed in such circumstances.

Where force is used in the prevention of crime or in arresting someone, the person using the force must consider if there are any viable alternatives, such as achieving compliance through their ability to communicate.

Additionally the recommendations of the Criminal Law Revision Committee (as it considered the criminal law on this subject) also raised the issues of force being used only when it is:

- Reasonable in the circumstances.

- An absolute necessity.

- The minimum amount necessary.

- Proportionate to the seriousness of the circumstances. (Also addressed in the *Human Rights Act 1998*.)

Human Rights Act 1998

2.22   The *Human Rights Act 1998* came into force in October 2000. Its purpose is to incorporate the various provisions contained in the European Convention of Human Rights (ECHR) into UK domestic law to ensure that the rights and freedoms of the individual are protected from unjustified interference by the State.

In simple terms, *section 6* of the 1998 Act states that it is unlawful for a 'public authority' to act in a way which is incompatible with a Convention right.

A public authority is defined very loosely and it will be a matter for interpretation as to what precisely is covered by the definition, and this appears to be widening with time. Some are obvious, for example; a police service, the Crown Prosecution Service, the NHS, local authorities, councils, and courts of law. Some are less so, and it is important to recognise that a private undertaking can be a public authority. The Lord Chancellor has identified Railtrack as an example of a body with mixed private and public functions and it would follow, for example, that a private security firm would be a public authority when managing contracted-out prison services, but would be acting privately when guarding private premises.

The *Human Rights Act 1998* has two basic purposes:

1. The rights and freedoms set out in the Act are actionable in the UK court system.

2. Courts and tribunals, public authorities and government ministers will have to act in a way that is compatible with the law of the ECHR. Failure to do so may be unlawful.

The most likely area where the *Human Rights Act 1998* will impact upon the issues of workplace violence is in the way that a 'public authority' treats the people involved in incidents. A person who works for a public authority is acting upon its behalf. There are four articles that could deal with this:

- Article 2 – the right to life

  Article 2 might be breached in the extremely rare event of someone dying as a result of physical force being used upon them. Exceptions to this Article include where the deprivation of life shall not be regarded as inflicted in contravention of the Article when it results from a use of force that is no more than absolutely necessary:

o   In defence of a person from unlawful violence.

o   In order to effect a lawful arrest or to prevent the escape of a person lawfully detained.

o   In action lawfully taken to quell a riot or insurrection.

The European Court of Human Rights has held that 'in keeping with the importance of this provision [the right to life] in a democratic society, the court must, in making its assessment, subject deprivation of life to the most careful scrutiny ... taking into consideration not only the actions of the agents of the State who actually administer force, but also all the surrounding circumstances including such matters as the planning and control of the actions under examination' (*McCann v United Kingdom (1995) 21 EHRR 97* at paragraph 150).

• Article 3 – absolute prohibition of torture, inhumane or degrading treatment

This is an absolute right and could possibly be breached by the use of force or restraint where is was unnecessary, where the level of force used is higher than was necessary or where a restraint is applied for a prolonged period where other options may have been viable.

• Article 5 – the right to liberty

This article could be breached where a person is detained against his will and where there is no basis in domestic law for such detention.

• Article 8 – the right to respect for private and family life

This includes respect for an individual's moral and physical integrity.

Some Convention rights are 'qualified rights' and contain clauses that enable a public authority to justifiably balance or restrict them in the 'public interest'. Articles 2, 3 and 5 are 'absolute rights' and cannot be interfered with in the public interest.

Use of force law in Scotland

2.23   The use of force law in Scotland is very similar to that in England. Scots common law allows force to be used to defend oneself, others and in some cases property (*Jones v HM Advocate 1989 SCCR 726*).

This has been further qualified: 'if a man sees another man being unlawfully attacked he is entitled to stop that unlawful attack' (Lord Wheatley in *HMA v Carson 1964 SLT 21*).

Persons other than police officers are also entitled to use reasonable force to detain those whom they see committing serious crimes. There must be good grounds for making a citizen's arrest and mere suspicion that another has committed an offence will not be enough. A private citizen is entitled to make an arrest without a warrant for a serious crime he has witnessed, or perhaps where he was the victim of the crime, or where he has information equivalent to personal observation, as when the fleeing criminal is pointed out to him by an eye witness (*Codona v Cardle 1989 SLT 791*).

Note: the common law of trespass does not exist in Scotland.

Other sector-specific legislation

2.24   Further legislation and bye laws exist that affect specific areas of work and include:

- Rail

    Bye laws cover trespass and common offences on the railway, and also include powers related to the use of force.

- Aviation

    Important legislation and guidance on the handling of disruptive passengers is contained in the:

    o   *Air Navigation Order 2000 (SI 2000/1562).*

    o   *Civil Aviation Act 1982.*

    o   Tokyo Convention.

    o   IATA Guidelines.

- Schools

    The *Education Act 1996* provides key powers on the issues of trespass [*section 547*] and pupil restraint [*section 550*].

- Mental health

    The *Mental Health Act 1983* carries powers of detention and use of force in certain circumstances.

- Football

    The *Football Offences Act 1991* provides powers to stewards and others in dealing with persons illegitimately on playing areas during a match (or adjacent area to which they to not have authority to be).

- Security

    Employees who are likely to become involved in the arrest of other persons such as thieves, also need to understand relevant sections of the *Police and Criminal Evidence Act 1984 (PACE).*

3 National Occupational Standards in Managing Work-related Violence

Background

3.1   The National Occupational Standards in Managing Work-related Violence have been developed very recently by the Employment National Training Organisation, which represents anyone with a concern for health and safety in the workplace. The work was funded by the Health and Safety Executive (HSE) as part of the work of the Psycho-social Issues Policy Unit to reduce the high number of assaults that occur in the workplace each year. The work was supported by the Institute of Conflict Management, who intend to use the Standards as a benchmark for their own activities. Other government departments such as the Department of Health, and the Department of Work and Pensions have also supported the work.

This chapter will outline what occupational standards are and how they can be used by organisations across the UK. It will then briefly outline the specific units of the National Occupational Standards in Managing Work-related Violence and the practical implications of the Standards for businesses and employers.

National Occupational Standards

3.2   There are a range of standards and benchmarks available to employers and others in the workplace, such as Investors in People, industry-specific inspection regimes and in-house quality assurance systems. These consider the whole organisation and the processes used to ensure the whole organisation delivers a good service. They are useful in benchmarking an organisation and providing guidance as to how the service or product can be improved.

In contrast, the National Occupational Standards describe what an individual must do to be competent in a particular task in any relevant workplace. An employer can choose to use both organisational benchmarks such as IiP and National Occupational Standards at the same time, to develop and improve the organisation.

Within the UK, National Occupational Standards are used in a range of settings to:

- Define good practice.

- Raise standards of practice.

- Encourage different agencies to take a common approach to a particular task.

- Provide protection for users/ customers of a particular service.

- Define what should be included in qualifications.

- Make requirements about appropriate qualifications for particular roles.

National Occupational Standards are developed by employers, employees, professional bodies, trade unions and other stakeholders in a process of consultation and consensus to reflect what people should be doing in the workplace. Quite often the process of developing the Standards leads to a debate in the sector about what is good practice and has the effect of raising practice as employers, employees, trade unions, professional bodies and customers/ service users consider what kind of service should be available. The Standards are outcome related, describing what the person should do rather than how they develop their competence. However, in order to be competent an individual needs to have some knowledge and this is reflected in the Standards, which include the underpinning knowledge needed to be competent.

National Occupational Standards (NOS) can be used by managers:

- to devise policies and procedures for their organisation;

- as a basis for analysing specific incidents;

- as a tool in planning how to approach a particular situation or activity;

- to appraise staff;

- to specify training outcomes.

It is hoped that the new Standards in Managing Work-related Violence will have an enormous impact upon the whole area of work-related violence across the UK. It has already been mentioned that there is a considerable lack of information about the problem and one of the difficulties has been the lack of a standardised approach to deal with the issues, a lack of information about incidents and about the effectiveness of risk reduction measures. For the first time, employers will be approaching the issues from the same position. This will lead to a greater sharing of best practice within and across the sectors. The reporting and recording processes will be more integrated and the subsequent information will lead a to a greater understanding of the whole area of work-related violence. This in turn will lead to more effective prevention and reduction measures.

NOS are also used by other groups in a variety of ways as follows:

- By employees and trade unions as a basis for making requirements on managers to improve practice in the workplace.

- By trainers as a basis for achieving certain objectives during training courses.

- By professional bodies and trade associations who may use the National Occupational Standards as a basis for their own standards, including membership and professional development.

- By awarding bodies as a basis for qualifications: from July 2002 all publicly funded qualifications in England must show how they relate to the relevant National Occupational Standards.

Practice and procedure across different sectors tends to develop from the unique standpoint that the particular organisation has towards dealing with an issue, client or service user. Organisations with a role that is primarily an enforcement one may differ in their approach from another organisation, involved in the same issue, which has a more supporting and caring role. For example, if social workers are intending to take children into care because they judge the children to be at risk they may request the support of the police in the event of any violence occurring. If the police and social workers take a different approach, perhaps giving the parents different information, there is a much greater likelihood of violence taking place. The National Occupational Standards will help people from a number of different agencies to have a shared language and work in more harmony with each other. By using these Standards to plan how they will go about the process and working together there is a much greater chance of being able to achieve the outcome – the child removed from the risk – without violence taking place.

National Occupational Standards as a basis for qualifications

3.3   Qualifications in England, Wales and Northern Ireland are regulated by the Qualifications and Curriculum Authority (QCA), and in Scotland by the Scottish Qualifications Authority (SQA). QCA/ SQA work with awarding bodies (such as City and Guilds, Edexcel, OCR) and National Training Organisations (NTOs)/ Sector Skills Councils in the development and implementation of qualifications. The NTOs/ Sector Skills Council represent the sector to devise the National Occupational Standards and a qualification structure for National Vocational Qualifications, showing what is judged to be essential for an individual in any particular role. National Vocational Qualifications (NVQs) (Scottish Vocational Qualifications in Scotland) are not specific to a particular employer, or region, and thus can be transferred from one employer to another, and between different counties within the UK. Some S/ NVQs are also recognised outside the UK. Increasingly NOS are being used as the basis for other qualifications, including those offered by individual awarding bodies.

Regulation and review of National Occupational Standards

3.4 NOS are developed by NTOs/ Sector Skills Councils in consultation with the people working in the sector. There are currently 73 NTOs, which are being replaced with a smaller number of Sector Skills Councils representing a wider range of occupational areas. Once Standards have been developed they are presented to the QCA/ SQA who consider:

- whether the Standards reflect practice across the whole of the UK;

- whether the Standards are written in a way that meets current requirements for NOS;

- whether the Standards can be used in qualifications.

A set of Standards is made up of a number of units, each unit reflecting a particular function which can be carried out by one person. Once these criteria have been satisfied the National Occupational Standards are approved, usually for a period of five years, after which they have be reviewed to ensure they continue to reflect any changes in practice.

National Occupational Standards in Managing Work-related Violence

3.5 In developing the Standards the priority was always to identify and minimise the causes of violence to prevent it arising, rather than developing competence in dealing with violent incidents. As a result the units follow an holistic approach that emphasises the role of managers in preventing violence rather than the role of individuals in defusing a situation once it has arisen.

These Standards will enable any employer to identify what they need to do to reduce the risk of violence occurring in their workplace, and to better manage such incidents when they do occur. The Standards provide a comprehensive checklist of actions which are appropriate in any setting.

Potential legal implications of National Occupational Standards

3.6 The new National Occupational Standards in Managing Work-related Violence provide employers with much needed clarity over what action a prudent employer is expected to take in preventing and managing violence. Health and Safety legislation has laid down the requirements upon employers to manage risk – including that of violence, but this has been in very general terms. The NOS now provides a much-needed framework that will guide employers, and also provide a means for measuring their response to the problem. The Standards will also be a useful benchmark for health and safety managers, internal and external inspectors, and the law courts when considering an employer's response to the risks faced in their workplace. For example, employers who are sued by employees for compensation resulting from a workplace violence incident are likely to find themselves in difficulties defending a claim if they have not followed the NOS (unless they have a good reason for saying why the NOS was not appropriate to their business).

The role of the Institute of Conflict Management (ICM)

3.7   The ICM has played a key role in the process of developing the NOS and is now working in partnership with key bodies in different sectors to provide guidance on their successful implementation. The ICM runs local and national events on this issue and also provides information and guidance on its web site at: www.conflictmanagement.org.

The ICM is taking a two-pronged approach to raising standards of training provision in this field by targeting both providers and purchasers. As purchasers develop their understanding of effective management and training approaches, they will be more discerning when reviewing the products and services on offer. This will in turn put pressure on the providers of these products and services to raise their standards.

The Institute also acts as a conduit for best practice on conflict management, and providers and purchasers alike can obtain numerous benefits from membership.

Catalogue of unit and element titles

3.8   There are eleven Units which make up the NOS in Managing Work-related Violence and they adhere to HSE's good practice and policy guidelines. These Units link to each other and in some places slightly overlap, but completion of all Units is not required or necessary to show competency in managing violence at work. These eleven Units may be used as part of other qualifications but it is unlikely that anyone would wish to achieve all the Units as they reflect a range of different roles.

The Units are copyright to the Employment NTO and purchasing details are given at **3.20**.

Unit W1: Assess the risk of violence to workers

3.9

W1.1   Identify the triggers of violence

W1.2   Assess the level of risks and prepare an action plan

W1.3   Review your assessment of risks

This Unit is about the skills and knowledge required for identifying triggers of violence, assessing the level of risks, planning and recommending action to help reduce that risk. To achieve the objectives of the Unit an individual will need to show any changes they have made as a result of a risk assessment.

The element W1.2 requires a person to:

- Identify those risks which can and cannot be eliminated.

- Assess the risks and prioritise them.

- Prepare an action plan on the implementation of the risk assessment to include recommendations on appropriate training for all workers, workers at most risk and new workers.

- Monitor changes which might produce new risks of violence.

Unit W1 provides a framework for one of the most important elements of any response to workplace violence – that of risk assessment. Employers have had to rely upon the approaches to risk assessment that have evolved through assessing the more tangible risks of machinery and dangerous substances. This has served reasonably well but as pointed out in CHAPTER 5 the assessment of risks for violence is unique and specific. Risks of violence are more unpredictable, less tangible and less passive because they inevitably involve an interaction with another person. This Unit will encourage health and safety managers, line managers and staff to approach the risk assessment from a workplace violence perspective and provide recommendations for risk reduction measures that are based on a more accurate assessment of the risks.

Unit W2: Develop an effective policy and procedures for minimising the risk of violence to your workers

3.10

W2.1   Develop a policy and procedures for managing work-related violence

W2.2   Review the effectiveness of the 'managing work-related violence' policy and procedures

This Unit is suitable for someone who is responsible for developing policies and procedures to minimise the risk of violence in the workplace. It shows the skills and knowledge required for developing an effective policy and procedures which specify the minimum acceptable standards for a safe working practice, and how to review the effectiveness of these policies.

Policy development in relation to workplace violence is a process that most organisations find difficult. Reflecting the problems and reality of the workplace in a policy is always fraught with charges that 'it's okay in theory, but it doesn't work in practice' and the policy often ends up as a forgotten document – pulled out and dusted off when there is a problem. In fact, CHAPTER 4 emphasises that a policy should be a working, live document that helps people to deal with this difficult and sometimes dangerous problem. Good policy formation will involve extensive consultation with everyone who is affected by the issue. It will clearly outline the organisation's stance on violence and provide practical and realistic guidance in its management. The Unit places much emphasis on the need to continuously review the effectiveness of policy and procedures through consultation with workers and to ensure best practice and adjustments are introduced as quickly as possible.

Unit W3: Implement policy and procedures to reduce the risk of violence at work

3.11

W3.1   Enable workers to maximise their safety and that of other people

W3.2   Review the implementation of policies and procedures to prevent violence at work

This Unit is suitable for the person who is responsible for implementing policies and procedures to reduce the risk of violence in the workplace. It shows the skills and knowledge required to ensure the measures and guidelines are in place for reducing violence at work, ensuring managers and workers follow procedures and are properly equipped to do so. The importance of effectively communicating key policy messages is highlighted.

The Unit refers specifically to policy on training and staff support following an incident, and these are explored in depth in CHAPTER 7 TRAINING and CHAPTER 9 POST-INCIDENT MANAGEMENT. It also reinforces the need for opportunities to be made for workers to prepare and practice procedures before they face difficult situations.

The second element shows what is necessary to review the implementation of procedures for preventing violence at work. It outlines the need to involve workers in this process, and in:

- Monitoring incidents and patterns.

- Measuring outcomes of training and identifying further needs.

- Reviewing and amending procedures as necessary.

Unit W4: Develop and maintain an effective management information system

3.12

W4.1 Develop a management information system for recording incidents of violence

W4.2 Maintain the system to monitor performance

This Unit describes how to produce a qualitative system of information to aid in the management of work-related violence and how to monitor incidents involving workers. It also describes how to use the system for producing reports and making it available for reviews.

This particular area is currently approached in widely differing ways – some very effective systems exist but many fail to record even the most basic information. The initial information from each incident and the information from the analysis of the collective data from all the incidents are both vital to informing the policy, procedures, practice, training and other risk reduction measures. Front line staff are best placed to understand the issues and good management data can unearth issues like 'hotspots', ineffective equipment and inappropriate practices which are not immediately apparent. This Unit highlights the importance of designing a system that provides quality management information that is informative on all aspects of policy and strategy. This vital area is explored in depth in CHAPTER 4 DEVELOPING AND IMPLEMENTING POLICY.

Unit W5: Promote a safe and positive working environment

3.13

W5.1 Develop plans to promote a safe and positive working environment

W5.2 Implement plans to promote a safe and positive working environment

This Unit is suitable for anyone responsible for promoting a positive working environment where workers feel safe from violence. It covers the skills and knowledge required to plan how to improve the culture at work by reviewing the current level of understanding on violence at work. It is also about producing plans to promote a safe and positive working environment, and providing opportunities for discussion and communication about violence at work. This should involve workers and others such as service users, ensuring shared understanding and two-way feedback. It is important to create an open 'no blame' learning environment and everyone, including senior managers, line managers and staff, can contribute to this.

Unit W6: Ensure your actions contribute to a positive and safe working environment

3.14

W6.1   Ensure your actions contribute to a positive and safe working environment

W6.2   Reduce the risk of violence in your working environment

This Unit is suitable for anyone at work, regardless of employment status, as everyone needs to ensure their actions contribute to a positive and safe working environment. It covers identifying where the risks are in a job role and the triggers that may escalate behaviour towards violence. It is also about understanding relevant organisational procedures, knowing what to do and how to carry out work in a calm and professional manner. There should be an awareness amongst everyone of their responsibilities in the work place, including working safely.

Policy, procedures and risk assessment are only part of the whole approach to dealing with workplace violence. The most important risk reduction measures lie, in the main, with the staff who are working directly with the public, clients, patients and service users. Individual approach, attitude, awareness of and recognition of increasing risks are all important to preventing and minimising violence and aggression. This comprehensive Unit highlights just how much workers can do to reduce the risk of conflict and violence, and how they can influence their safety through:

- Increased awareness.

- Adopting safe practice.

- Delivering a good service.

Unit W7: Protect yourself from the risk of violence at work

3.15

W7.1   Help to de-escalate a potentially violent situation

W7.2   Review the incident for recording and monitoring purposes

This Unit is suitable for people who finds themselves in a situation where they need to calm down a potentially violent situation at work. It covers calming a potentially dangerous situation by minimising actions or words that may trigger violent behaviour and by showing respect for people, their property and rights. It is about responding to a situation by trying to calm it down and, when appropriate, leaving a threatening situation safely. It is also about reviewing the incident for recording and monitoring purposes.

The areas outlined in this Unit will require the development of specific skills, largely through appropriate training. The design and delivery of training in this regard is covered in depth within CHAPTER 7.

The second element of the Unit places considerable importance on the need to reflect and report on the incident, and to draw lessons from it to reduce risk in the future. It also refers to the need to make use of available support. These issues are covered in CHAPTER 9.

Unit W8: Respond to work-related violent incidents

3.16

W8.1   Resolve a violent situation

W8.2   Follow up procedures for evaluating violent incidents

This Unit is for people who work in an occupation which requires them to respond to a violent situation. This could for example include security or response teams, or managers expected to take control of incidents.

It includes taking immediate and appropriate action, when an incidence of violence occurs, to reduce risk to one self and other individuals. It is also about recording events and reviewing actions and those of other people in order to help prevent further similar incidents.

The Unit acknowledges the need for physical intervention in certain circumstances where it is both reasonable and necessary. Guidance and training is essential in workplaces where staff are likely to need physical interventions, and this is covered further in CHAPTER 7. Reporting and recording incidents is covered in CHAPTER 5 RISK ASSESSMENT AND REPORTING.

Unit W9: Support individuals involved in violent incidents at work

3.17

W9.1   Provide immediate support

W9.2   Ensure continuing support is available

This Unit is for people who are responsible for supporting workers/employees who have been involved in violent incidents at work. It covers their role in providing the appropriate support to those affected by a violent incident at work. The support should be consistent with statutory regulations and policies and procedures laid down by the organisation. It is about ensuring support is available immediately, as well as in the short and long term.

Support provided after an incident is usually dependent upon the resources and culture of the organisation concerned. Some organisations provide a comprehensive response to supporting their employees both immediately after an incident and the sometimes difficult days that follow. Other organisations may offer very little support. The quality of the support provided will depend on the quality and skills of the individual's line manager. The Standards give a comprehensive framework for effective post-incident support and provide for the responsibilities of managers in this context. CHAPTER 9 explores the training needs of managers across the whole area of support for staff who have been through an incident of work-related violence.

Unit W10: Investigate and evaluate incidents of violence at work

3.18

W10.1   Investigate incidents of violence at work

W10.2   Recommend measures to reduce incidents of violence

This Unit is for people who investigate incidents of violence at work. It covers responding promptly to complaints of violence regardless of the size of the incident and recording events accurately in accordance with organisational requirements. It is also about assessing the causes of the incidents, evaluating and recommending any action in order to prevent further incidents.

Learning from an incident of workplace violence is a crucial part of the whole response to this issue. Effective investigation of the circumstances can provide vital information about immediate ongoing risks that need to be dealt with as well as longer-term issues and reflected in policy, procedures or training. 'Investigation' is also a very sensitive area and needs to be carried out from a standpoint of learning rather then blame. The Standards provide a framework that will help organisations to carry out sensitive, professional and thorough reviews of incidents of workplace violence and these issues are covered in CHAPTER 9.

Unit W11: Ensure effective communications following an incident of violence at work

3.19

W11.1   Brief relevant people following an incident of violence at work

W11.2   Make positive use of external communications following an incident of violence at work

This Unit is for the person responsible for ensuring that both internal and external communications are handled effectively after an incident of violence at work. It covers the skills and knowledge required for ensuring that the necessary information is communicated to the relevant people in a professional manner whilst maintaining appropriate confidentiality.

Sometimes, it is important to share the details of an incident of workplace violence quite quickly within the organisation. It may be that a particular work practice is exposed as being dangerous or perhaps a particular group of individuals are causing a danger to staff. It is important to get such information to the appropriate people quickly. There may also be external communication needs following an incident, for example, media interest. In particular there is a need to protect both employees and the organisation from the harm that such interest can sometimes cause. This Unit provides a framework for internal and external communication in both of these types of situation. CHAPTER 8 INCIDENT MANAGEMENT and CHAPTER 9 POST-INCIDENT MANAGEMENT are particularly relevant to this Unit.

How to purchase the Standards

3.20   The National Occupational Standards in Managing Work-related Violence may be purchased from the Employment NTO (website: www.empnto.co.uk; telephone: 0116 2519 727).

4 Developing and Implementing Policy

Introduction

4.1   In the past, the most common approach to workplace violence has been to include it within the general management of health and safety within an organisation. There is now a growing recognition that incidents of work-related violence have increased significantly over the last decade. The more enlightened approach is to treat workplace violence as a specific issue, separate from the general health and safety issues within an organisation. This is reinforced by the introduction of National Occupational Standards specifically relating to the management of work-related violence (see CHAPTER 3).

There is also a growing recognition that the problem exists to some degree within most customer-facing organisations, not just the 'traditional' sectors of security and policing. Most startling, perhaps, is the increasing level of workplace aggression and violence that is being directed at those people who have elected to work in caring roles within our society. Nurses, doctors, ambulance crews, social workers, benefit officers, teachers, fire crews and even the clergy are all experiencing an increasing risk of being abused or assaulted whilst trying to carry out their roles. There are people who will readily turn their frustration with poor service, late trains, delayed flights and inconsiderate driving into a personal and physical attack on front line staff who are generally trying to provide the best service they can. Even in the recognised risk sectors of enforcement, security and policing, there is a greater risk of incidents turning into violent confrontations and a reluctant but growing acceptance that this type of behaviour 'goes with the job'.

Despite these trends, there is still a strong view that abusive or violent behaviour towards people who are trying to do their job should not be tolerated. In March 2000, The Health and Safety Commission (HSC) embarked on a three-year partnership programme to achieve a 10% reduction in work-related violence by the end of the programme. Much violence goes unreported and increased awareness and education is actually resulting in an increase in reporting in many organisations and sectors. This has in fact been the case with the NHS Zero Tolerance Campaign.

Health and safety legislation demands that the risks of workplace violence are properly assessed and effective measures put in place to minimise those risks. In any organisation that has workers at risk from such violence, a comprehensive and workable policy is the cornerstone for building an effective response to work-related violence in an organisation. Surprisingly, many organisations that fit into this category are lagging way behind in their corporate response to the issue. Such complacency is dangerous – if an organisation is unfortunate enough to be placed under external scrutiny as the result of an incident involving workplace violence, the first thing that will be requested is a copy of the policy, along with training records and incident reports.

This chapter provides a practical guide to developing a policy that is specifically targeted at dealing with the issue of work-related violence in an organisation. This is followed by a discussion on how to develop a written strategy for implementing the policy; this includes how to communicate the policy internally to the workforce and externally to customers, clients and the general public. Finally, there is guidance on ways of measuring and monitoring the effects of the policy, bench-marking progress and working with other agencies.

The following model illustrates the process:

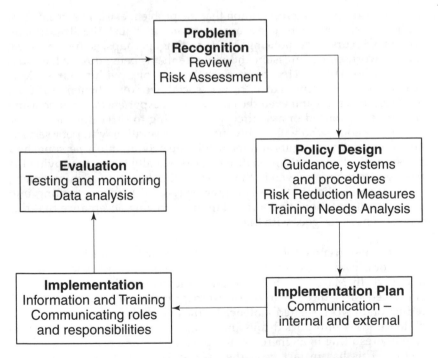

Figure 4.1: Model for policy development

Problem recognition

4.2   It is important to remember that developing and writing the policy is only the starting point. Equally important, and perhaps the most difficult part, is the implementation of the policy and measures that flow from it. Many violence policies fail to have an impact because they lack a written implementation strategy and plan, and a workplace violence co-ordinator (which could be part of a manager's role).

It is also important to recognise the policy as a living, changing entity. Once implemented, the processes, procedures, equipment, training and incidence of violence need to be monitored, analysed and evaluated. Revision and review of the policy will flow from this, together with consequent changes to the procedures, guidance, equipment and training. This should happen on a continuous basis, maintaining a proactive and problem-solving approach to the ever-changing risks associated with work-related violence and aggression.

The starting point for a policy is the recognition that there is an issue to be addressed. Ideally, this should be realised through a proactive corporate approach towards the whole issue of welfare and safety of staff. However, all too often, the problem is recognised as a reaction to increasing staff turnover, one too many incidents of serious injury, or litigation from an employee who has been seriously hurt. Whichever way it is recognised, it is important that a strong recognition of the problem is stated and communicated to the employees. Even before a policy is written and introduced, it is important that employees are assured that work-related violence is recognised as an important issue and that something is going to be done about it.

The most important first step is to define what 'workplace violence' means within the organisation. Most organisations use the definition offered by the Health and Safety Executive (HSE):

> 'Any incident in which a person is abused, threatened, or assaulted in circumstances relating to their work'.

This is a very wide definition, which covers a whole range of possible scenarios. Importantly, it includes incidents where someone uses abusive language or behaviour that does not amount to a threat of or actual physical assault. It also covers incidents that might occur when people are not actually at work; for example, being followed home or confronted when arriving at or leaving work. Adopting this definition has several benefits. In particular, it develops a common language and approach across different organisations and helps to benchmark against similar organisations in the same industry sector.

It should be noted that this definition does not only cover violence from service users and outsiders (ie those unconnected with the service who employees come into contact with) but also includes 'internal' incidents involving managers, supervisors and co-workers. All such incidents should be reported.

Bullying and harassment unfortunately does occur in some workplaces and can have a significant impact on an individual's well being and the organisational performance. Without diminishing the importance of preventing and confronting such behaviour, it is not within the remit of this book to cover these issues. The management strategy for tackling the more 'covert' internal issues tends to differ from that designed to address overt violence and that presented by service users and outsiders. Bullying, harassment and discrimination issues therefore deserve a dedicated policy and management strategy.

One further definition of importance is that used by the British Crime Survey (BCS):

'All assaults or threats which occurred while the victim was working and were perpetrated by a member of the public'.

With the high incidence of under-reporting the BCS is probably the most important single source of information about trends in work-related violence across England and Wales. It includes information about incidents that have not been officially reported within the organisation or to the police, and the survey also gathers information about the fear of violence at work. The HSC is using the BCS 2000 figures as a benchmark for their three-year programme to reduce the incidence of work-related violence.

Developing the policy is not a 'paper exercise'. It can easily be viewed in this way and given to someone in the human resources department or to the health and safety manager as a project, with the recipient expected to come up with a policy in a couple of weeks. Good policy is based on a sound understanding of all the issues, gained from a variety of sources. When starting from scratch, the most effective way of achieving this is to conduct a full review of the problem.

Conducting a review

Who, what, where, when, why and how?

4.3   The purpose of a review is to establish:

- the nature and extent of the problem;
- the specific roles that are at risk;
- the nature of the risks;
- the solutions to minimise the risks identified.

In simple terms, this is trying to establish:

- *Who* is at risk?

- *What* is the nature of the risk?

- *When* and *where* is the risk presented?

- *Why* does the risk occur?

- Ultimately – *how* can the risk can be eliminated or minimised?

Collaboration

4.4   An important element in the eventual success of such a review will be the approach adopted from the outset. 'Reviews' of any sort can be seen by employees variously as a threat, a waste of time, a typical useless management activity, snooping and 'trying to catch us out'. The great thing about this review is that its intention is primarily to ensure employees operate in an environment where risks from work-related violence are minimised, and only the most hardened cynic will claim it is about management protecting their backs. Here is a fairly unique opportunity to involve employees, managers, supervisors and union representatives who will be enthusiastic to help achieve the aims. Collaboration is an essential element in gaining the buy-in across all the interested parties, which is essential for the successful implementation of a policy. Equally, not one person, role or department has a monopoly of knowledge in relation to the issues; front line personnel are meeting and dealing with these problems every day.

Sources of information

4.5   To carry out an effective review, there are a variety of sources from which data and information can be gathered. These include:

- Generic risk assessment of specific roles.

- Interviews, observation, focus groups and questionnaires.

- Analysis of data.

Generic violence risk assessment of specific roles

4.6   The people who face the customers, clients, patients and public every day are best placed to identify and understand the risks they face from violence and aggression, and risk assessment of roles is a statutory requirement under health and safety legislation. A good, generic violence risk assessment of each role will identify the inherent risks associated with carrying out that role. Risk assessment should include a physical assessment of working environments and take into account conditions such as lone working and visiting clients/ customers in their homes. The assessment will identify things like training requirements, safety equipment needed, and specific working practices that need to be adopted. Risk assessment is dealt with in more detail in CHAPTER 5 where a risk assessment tool is included.

Interviews, observation, focus groups and questionnaires

4.7 It is also important to gather views from front line staff about the effects that the risks of workplace violence have upon them. It is important to remember that the perception of risk is as important as the reality, and organisations have a responsibility to deal with the fear of being subjected to violence and aggression, as well as the actual risk of violence.

The information can be gathered through informal interviews with affected staff, focus groups of staff from a particular role or through a questionnaire which is designed to extract the appropriate information. Often, a combination of these techniques is used. The design, implementation and analysis of questionnaires, interviews and focus groups is a specialised process and this should be achieved through someone who knows what they are doing.

There are issues around confidentiality and individuals often fear their views will 'get back to management'. Confidentiality must be guaranteed, be evident in the procedure and be completely respected in practice. It is helpful if someone who is perceived to be 'independent' of management conducts this part of the review.

This consideration is also important if it is decided to observe employees in their normal working environment. A great deal of important information can be gleaned from observing how people approach and interact with customers, clients and members of the public. However, it is an extraordinarily sensitive area and needs to be carried out in an open and honest way. It is very difficult to carry out an observation using 'in-house' personnel without people feeling that they are being 'checked on'. It is often accepted much more readily when carried out by an external consultant who can engage an individual in the work setting to talk and ask questions about his or her role whilst also observing the issues and interactions that take place.

Analysis of data

4.8 The data available will vary according to the nature of the organisation and the sophistication of the reporting and recording procedures available. In the best case, a dedicated reporting system will inform about not only the number of incidents of violence and aggression but also information about times of day, locations, nature of injuries, frequency and types of injury, roles most at risk, and so on.

The reality will be probably somewhat different. However, useful information can be gained from a variety of sources including reported incidents and accidents, staff appraisals, exit interviews with staff who are leaving, staff and customer satisfaction surveys and sickness reporting and patterns. It may well be that a great deal of useful information is sitting quietly in the human resources department waiting to be discovered! The intention will be to build a reporting system that will provide specific data to inform the response to workplace violence; this is covered in more detail in CHAPTER 5.

The review – 'do-it-yourself' or bring someone in?

4.9   The decision about whether to use internal resources to conduct a review or bring in an external consultant is important and needs some careful consideration. There are pro's and con's to each and they need to be weighed properly to ensure the decision is the right one for the organisation.

Do-it-yourself

4.10   The most compelling reason for choosing to 'do-it-yourself' is usually cost. A firm of consultants may charge a daily rate anywhere between £500 and £1,500 and this can run up a sizeable outlay. A thorough review will take several days to conduct.

It is important to fully appreciate the specialist knowledge and skills required to properly review the risks associated with workplace violence. A lot of help, advice and assistance is available on the internet from sources like the HSE, trade unions and other specialist organisations – see APPENDIX for a list of recommended resources. It is essential to fully research the general issues and the areas specific to the particular sector. It is also pointless to 're-invent the wheel'. It is likely that another organisation in the sector has undertaken this process successfully and may be willing to share their experience and best practice.

The issue of confidentiality and fear of 'management reprisal' has been mentioned already. Sadly, warranted or otherwise, this is a real worry raised by many employees and will have a detrimental impact on the accuracy of any data unless it can be fully negated. This can also be linked to the specialist knowledge required to properly construct and design interviews, focus groups and questionnaires. It looks easy, but very simple mistakes in design are often made by 'enthusiastic amateurs', which completely flaw the data. If the organisation is to go down this road then it is important to seek specialist advice about design. There may be a research or performance measurement department that can help, or it may be appropriate to approach the local university; they often have research students who need 'live' projects to work on and who will be able to design and perhaps conduct the research.

Checklist

'Do-it-yourself' review

❏ How well equipped is the organisation to conduct a review of risks associated with workplace violence?

❏ What level of research is needed to bring the organisation up to speed on the issues and problems?

❏ How can the issues of confidentiality and 'mistrust' that might exist be overcome?

❏ What generic risk assessments exist for roles within the organisation and do they recognise workplace violence?

❏ What data is available which can be analysed to provide useful information about the risks of workplace violence?

❏ What help might be available from other organisations and institutions?

Bring someone in

4.11 A good external consultant will have a lot of experience and expertise in this area but will generally be relatively expensive. For the fee, they will be expected to conduct the review in its entirety and the review and resulting recommendations will provide an effective solution which will make staff feel safer and protect the organisation from litigation. Spending money on engaging external 'experts' sends a strong message to employees about how seriously the issue is being taken by the organisation. This extra investment is justified in that an external consultant has specialist knowledge, experience and expertise in conducting reviews into workplace violence.

It is also useful to recognise that many external providers and consultants are willing to give discounts to organisations to secure their long-term business. This may also extend to undertaking preparatory work such as a review – or at least assisting with the design and development of policy – at no charge.

There are many providers ranging from small 'sole trader' companies through to larger organisations who offer 'complete solutions'. It is important to check their credentials – not just as training providers but as consultants who have the expertise to conduct properly designed research and analysis. They should be able to demonstrate their previous record in this area and outline their research methodology and data analysis process.

The most effective way to check credentials is to ask for the details of clients for whom they have completed reviews and then contact such clients to find out what they thought of the quality of the work and services provided.

The checklist below provides a guide to the questions that should be asked of an external consultant to help gauge their ability to meet an organisation's requirements. This is not exhaustive and it is important that questions specific to the company's needs are asked as well.

Checklist

Bringing someone in

❑ What evidence can the external consultant provide of their expertise in the field of reviewing workplace violence?

❑ What do the other organisations that have worked with the external consultant say about the service?

❑ What methodology will the external consultant use to identify the issues and risks of workplace violence in the organisation?

❑ How will the external consultant develop their understanding of the business and organisation?

❑ What professional qualification/ development do the reviewers have?

Essential elements for a successful review

4.12   The approach to take to a review will depend very much upon the organisation, the availability of resources and the support received from senior managers. The review may be conducted in-house or through an external consultant, or perhaps a combination of both. Whatever the circumstances, the following provides a checklist of the essential elements to bear in mind when conducting a review of an organisation's approach to dealing with issues of work-related violence.

Developing policy – Review checklist

What's currently in existence?

❑ Who are the interested parties and what can they bring to the review process?

❑ Is there any current policy, guidance or advice in relation to workplace violence?

❑ What information is recorded about incidents of violence on staff?

❑ What measures are currently in place to minimise the risk of violence towards staff? Is it possible to gauge their effectiveness?

❑ Is any training offered in the organisation to help staff manage conflict and aggression in their roles?

❑ What initiatives, best practice and guidance are available to help with the issues specific to this business sector?

Generic violence risk assessment of roles

❑ Are generic risk assessments in existence for all roles that carry a risk of violence or aggression?

❑ Do they take account of role responsibilities that increase risk – such as enforcement duties, delivering 'unwelcome news' like benefit reduction etc?

❑ Do the risk assessments take account of environment and working conditions, such as interview rooms, reception areas, home visiting and lone working?

Gathering information

❑ Include a selection of employees who work in vulnerable roles, management and first line supervision and union representatives.

❑ Decide on methodology required to gather required information – interviews, focus groups, workplace observation, questionnaires.

❑ Consider issues of confidentiality, mistrust and perceived 'checking' on the workforce.

❑ How will the information be recorded so that it can be usefully analysed?

Analysing data

❑   What data is available to help identify risks of workplace violence?

❑   Does this organisation keep records of incidents, complaints, accidents and injuries? Can they be tracked back to gain information about the circumstances?

❑   Are there records of staff turnover, broken down into roles? Are exit interviews conducted with staff who leave?

❑   Are there records of sickness – particularly stress related?

❑   Analyse the information – looking for patterns, trends, hotspots and unusual correlations which might help to pin point areas of concern.

❑   Reviewing previous, current or pending litigation involving aggression and violence to staff.

Case Study – external review

4.13

Hamish Allan Centre, Glasgow City Council

The Hamish Allan Centre is concerned with providing accommodation and support for the homeless and operates rough sleeping initiatives, supported accommodation, hostels and multi-agency projects. Chief Housing Officer, Ian Robertson, recognised the difficult circumstances of homeless persons and the challenges that his staff faced as a result of these. The sensitivity and complex nature of the problems led to external specialists being commissioned to undertake a comprehensive review that included:

● The nature and extent of the risks faced by staff.

● The underlying causes of conflict and violence.

● Risk reduction measures.

● Training needs.

The review proved to be fundamental in establishing an accurate understanding of the existing situation and in shaping the resulting policy, strategy and training. The reviewers spent time in the working environment – often late at night – and staff could see that the problem was being taken seriously, that their experience was being respected, and that something positive was being done to create a safer environment for staff and clients. The review proved to be fundamental in achieving shared understanding and 'buy in' to the training and change process.

Designing the policy

Consultation and collaboration

4.14   The review will have probably produced a large amount of information and often, at this stage, more questions than answers. It is useful to consider who will be able to help make sense of the information and make some of the important decisions about the content of the policy. It is time to set up a working party or committee.

It is important that this group is made up of people who are informed about the issues and understand the practical implications of the decisions that are made. For example, it is quite common for an organisation to include a 'walk away' or 'don't touch' policy in their guidance on dealing with a potentially violent situation. This may be motivated by the view that 'our people won't get hurt if they walk away from it'. The difficulty is that in the reality of the workplace there are practical implications to a 'don't touch' policy. An employee has a right to defend himself or herself from attack. If the person is employed in some sort of 'enforcement role', perhaps checking that someone has a ticket or keeping order in a night-club, then what do they do if the customer or client fails to comply? What does one do if a colleague is being attacked? Does it mean, for instance, an elderly lady who needs a bit of support should not be touched? What if someone needs first-aid? The point here is that the policy needs to be framed by people who have the responsibility to make the decisions, but also are in touch with the realities of the workplace environment and can frame policy which takes into account these various issues.

In practice, such a group will probably exist for the general health and safety issues in the form of a health and safety committee or group. It is almost impossible to second-guess the variety of organisational structures that exist and therefore general principles are offered in the following model to achieve the most effective group (see figure 4.2 below).

In this model, there is a direct link through the practitioner group to the workplace issues and to the executive group who have ultimate responsibility for the policy. The working group makes the actual decisions.

In the more traditional 'hierarchical' organisations (and many organisations still operate this way), the culture expects that policy is driven from the 'top' down. The senior managers make the policy, the middle managers translate it into practice and the line managers and staff put it into practice. In our model, this has been turned 'upside down' to emphasise that the people who know most about the problems, and the solutions, are those who face them every day and therefore the practitioner group should drive the policy formation. The working group should translate this into workable policies, guidelines, practices and training solutions. The executive group should provide support, guidance

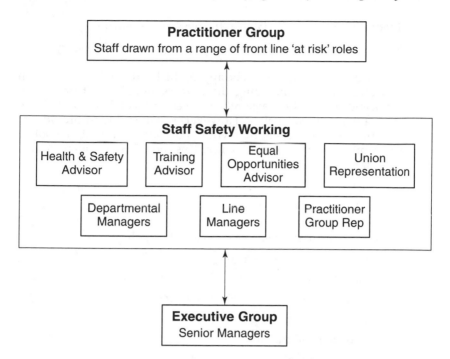

Figure 4.2: Model for effective policy development group

and advice and, ultimately, take responsibility for the policy. In this way, the front line staff have ownership of the issues from the beginning and have been fully involved in the creation of the solution. This will help considerably in the important process of putting the policy into practice.

Writing the policy

4.15   The policy needs to be:

- Informed – making use of information from the review process, consultation and analysis of data.

- Comprehensive – yet able to deliver simple clear messages to managers, staff and service users.

- Written in supportive terms (many policies tend to set out in lengthy terms what staff are not allowed to do, and the sanctions they will face).

- Informative – setting out the actions staff can take and then supporting them with post-incident procedures to follow.

- Lawful – taking into account relevant legislation including health and safety law and use of force.

- Tactically sound – is it viable in the work environment?

- Regularly reviewed and updated or changed where necessary.

There are many ways that this can be approached and it will depend upon many different factors, including the organisational structure, policy framework and culture. Consequently, it is very difficult here to lay down a template for the 'ideal' policy. However, it is possible to provide an outline of the areas of content that would normally be found in a policy aimed at minimising workplace violence. This should be considered as the minimum standard.

Policy content

4.16   These are the basic elements of an effective policy:

- Purpose.
- Scope and definitions.
- Who the policy affects and their specific responsibilities.
- Risk assessment, reporting and review process.
- Risk reduction and training.
- Response to incidents:
  - Incident management.
  - Post-incident management.
- Reporting.
- Involvement of other agencies and sanctions.
- Maintenance.
- Communication strategy.
- Policy review and revision.

Purpose

4.17   This part of the policy sets out the context and aims, and expresses the corporate values that support the existence of the policy. It is good practice to include a foreword from a senior manager who has the responsibility for the safety and welfare of staff. It sends a positive message and underlines the senior level commitment.

Scope and definitions

4.18   This part of the policy defines what is meant by 'workplace violence'. The HSE definition is recommended. This section should state clearly what is included within the policy and what is not; for example, violence towards staff by the public is covered by this policy –internal conflicts and bullying are not as a separate policy exists for these issues.

Who the policy affects

4.19   This part of the policy considers who is affected by the policy and identifies these individuals' specific roles and responsibilities in relation to the policy where appropriate.

The following could be affected:

- Victims and potential victims.
- Staff, supervisors and managers.
- Contractors and their staff.
- Key departments such as health and safety, and training.
- Trade unions.
- Customers/ service users / general public.
- Offenders and potential offenders.
- Witnesses.
- The media.

Risk assessment, reporting and review process

4.20   This part of the policy outlines the risk assessment process and requirements, together with clear expectations of managers and staff with regard to recording, classification and monitoring of incidents. This is covered in more detail in CHAPTER 5.

The risk assessment and review process will inform the risk reduction strategy.

Risk reduction and training

4.21   Risk reduction is at the heart of the policy and underpins the whole point of its existence. This is the part of the policy that outlines the measures that are to be taken to minimise the risks identified.

The key elements of risk reduction will be:

- advice, guidance, and procedures aimed at safer working practices;
- equipment and design of the working environment;
- improved service delivery and reduction in triggers of violence;
- training and development in handling conflict and potentially violent situations.

This section includes the approach to identifying and prioritising training needs, and for implementing and evaluating training. The violence Training Needs Analysis is covered in detail in CHAPTER 7.

Risk reduction will also identify special areas of risk and provide role-specific reduction measures. A good example is the lone worker who, in addition to the generic measures, may need extra equipment (eg mobile phone, attack alarm), special working practices (eg scheduled 'call in' procedures) and special training (eg personal security and safety awareness, exit strategies etc).

Response to incidents

4.22   The response will typically cover two key areas:

1.   Incident management

This part of the policy outlines the procedures that managers and staff are required to follow should a violent incident occur, and provides clarity on roles, responsibilities and communications. It also includes communications with other agencies such as police, security and media. It should state the position with regard to use of physical intervention and the provision of appropriate guidance and training.

2.   Post-incident management

This part of the policy clearly defines post-incident management procedures including reporting requirements, operational support, and immediate and longer-term staff support. It should also state the responsibilities of line managers and their health and safety and occupational health functions, and the feedback and learning process. This section should also declare the extent of the commitment of the organisation to staff welfare.

Also included within the section should be the requirements for rehearsal and testing of the incident and post-incident management procedures. The position on prosecution could be included here or under 'involvement with other agencies'.

Involvement of other agencies and sanctions

4.23   The *Crime and Disorder Act 1998* placed a legal requirement on local authorities and the police to co-operate with other bodies such as healthcare trusts, to formulate and implement crime and disorder strategies. Organisations are more likely to secure resources for tackling violent crime if they can produce evidence of recurring problems to these local crime and disorder partnerships.

This part of the organisation policy will outline guidance with regard to the involvement of other agencies such as the police and local authorities in terms of what they need from the organisation and what can be expected from them. It should also outline the stance on prosecution and the options available including legal/ financial support for employees. Also, where appropriate, the policy and guidance concerning exclusion and withdrawal of services should be included.

Maintenance

4.24   To alter behaviour, a policy must become part of the fabric of the organisation. Messages need to be consistent and threaded in at every opportunity. Performance indicators need to be established and managers held accountable for ensuring that breaches of policy and guidance are addressed. For example, what happens if medical staff do not attend violence and aggression training for staff working in an accident and emergency department. These issues should be outlined and addressed in the policy.

Communication strategy

4.25   This part of the policy states the corporate position with regard to internal and external publicity, and identifies key messages/ statements to be promoted. It should also include a strategy for managing media attention following an incident.

Policy review and revision

4.26   This part of the policy establishes a monitoring and review process that allows periodic re-evaluation of the strategy and policy. It builds in a feedback loop with each element of the strategy.

Implementation plan

4.27   Many violence prevention policies fail to create change as they lack a strategy for making it happen. An effective approach is to develop a concise policy document – approved by the relevant parties – with an accompanying written implementation strategy. This strategy document should include a detailed project plan outlining what will be done by whom and by when.

This is not just about letting the workforce know about the policy. Implementation is about making the policy happen. It includes educating people about new processes and procedures, ensuring managers understand and monitor new practices, introducing and using new equipment, and setting up and running a programme of training and development. There are many things to consider here, not least the fact that it is likely to involve change – and change is always difficult to implement.

Dealing with change

4.28   It is easy to change something such as a policy or procedure, but it does not necessarily result in things being done differently. True change or 'transition' is harder to achieve as it requires changes in attitude and behaviour, and this is especially so with the management of violence. Many organisations have policies covered in dust in their filing cabinets that are unlikely to have made any difference whatsoever in tackling the problem.

There are, however, two very positive aspects present which will help in the change process. First of all, the whole subject is directly concerned with making the workplace safer and therefore most people will start with a positive view of any changes. Secondly, if care has been taken to fully involve front line staff in the review and policy formation process there will already be considerable ownership of the new policy. Managing a 'positive' change can be achieved quite successfully by understanding the likely feelings that people who are affected by it will go through.

Initial enthusiasm

4.29   This is highly influenced by the way that the change is communicated. Each person will interpret the message in their own way and see the possibilities from their point of view. Initial views are likely to be that the introduction of a policy for dealing with workplace violence is a good thing and will have positive benefits. It is important to be as clear as possible in these first communications.

Creeping doubts

4.30   Different interpretations begin to circulate and people start to match these against their own expectations. The picture becomes less rosy as the different perceptions and expectations become clear and people realise that they may need to change the way they do things. The sorts of things that will begin to sow some seeds of doubt are: 'There's going to be a lot more form filling', 'Another course I've got to go on', 'This just seems to be an exercise in the management watching their backs'.

Seeking clarification

4.31   'Creeping doubts' result in people checking out their different perceptions, both privately and publicly, until they achieve a degree of collective clarity and come to a more realistic view of the changes. This stage is achieved more quickly if management deals both honestly and openly with all the issues and questions raised. It is a good idea to prepare for this phase and provide forums through workshops, briefings, intranet sites and 'frequently asked questions' to help people get the right answers to their anxieties.

Realistic enthusiasm

4.32   This takes people back to their initial point of view, but now they have a shared view of the change and are much more aware of the overall picture and the real implications involved.

Achieving the change

4.33   The change is achieved successfully for everyone concerned.

Adoption of change

4.34   Another point about change is that people will 'come on board' the change process at different stages, and if it is possible to identify how this happens, it is then also possible to target the people who will help the process along. The following model shows the general pattern that happens when change is introduced to a group of people.

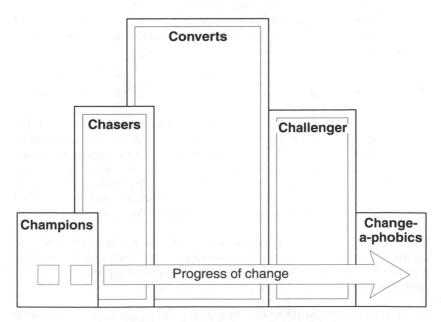

Figure 4.3: Adoption of change

Champions

4.35   Few in numbers, 'champions' are prepared to stick their neck out and will probably have volunteered to be part of the working group at the start up. Watch out for the individual who may have their own agenda – some people are interested in changing the status quo for their own ends and may be less interested in the change being proposed.

Chasers

4.36   'Chasers' are the early adopters who will quickly follow the champions. This may be because they quickly see the benefits of the change, or because they wish to emulate the champions. Watch for those who just like to be involved in change for its own sake (Change-a-holics).

Converts

4.37   This is the largest group. 'Converts' need some convincing and they will look for firm evidence that the change will produce benefits.

Challengers

4.38   'Challengers' are the people who care a lot about the status quo or have a strong stake in the outcome of the change. They need to be able to see the positive and specific outcomes of the change. They will probe and question until they are convinced. Convince them, and success is almost guaranteed.

Change-a-phobics

4.39   This group will not be won over, no matter how convincing the evidence is. 'Change-a-phobics' are the 'die-hard' cynics. They are usually small in number and can be very damaging if they manage to influence the other groups, particularly the converts who will 'sit on the fence'. Although one needs to be aware of these individuals, it is important not to be distracted by them; their resistance will wane once they recognise that the 'critical mass' of employees has embraced the changes.

In practice, the champions are the people who have helped the policy to be formed. They understand the issues and can both quickly sell the positive benefits and deal with the legitimate fears and problems that the staff raise.

The 'target' group should be the challengers. They may seem to be a thorn in the side of the organisation because they are the people who will always ask the awkward and difficult questions in meetings, focus groups and briefings. However, if their queries can be answered fully and to their satisfaction then it demonstrates that the policy is sound. If this cannot be achieved, then another look at the issue is called for. Convince the challengers and policy will be successfully implemented. Ideally some challengers will have been included in the early practitioner and working groups.

Communication

4.40   How the policy is communicated is absolutely vital to the success of its implementation. There are two aspects to this – internal communication to the people who work within the organisation, and external communication to the people who make up the clients, service users and the general public.

Internal communication

4.41   As always this will depend upon the structure, size and nature of the particular organisation. If it has a department that deals with communication and the media, their help will be invaluable. There are some factors that will help to make the communication process successful.

Plan

4.42   Don't assume it will just happen. Thought needs to be given to the target audience, the communication structures in the organisation and how to make the information accessible – particularly to workers who don't have easy access to channels like computers and email. Through the careful integration and timing of each element of the policy its impact can be maximised and successful transition will be more likely.

Policy launch

4.43   It is much more positive if people recognise the start of a new process. It marks the point when the changes begin and can have a very positive effect on the way people accept the new practices. It also allows use of a 'count down' period to both keep people informed of the progress and to reinforce the positive aspects of what is being developed for them.

Workplace briefings

4.44   Front line managers should be given a full understanding of the policy first, and then should communicate this to their staff. This has a greater impact because the messages are coming from someone who is directly in touch with their workplace and its issues and problems. It is important to distil key messages from the policy in communications with staff, and for these to be further reinforced in training.

Easy access 'help desk'

4.45   A system is needed where people can quickly have their queries, worries and doubts dealt with. Modern technology makes this much easier with intranet sites where 'frequently asked questions' can be posted and email queries can be quickly dealt with. This should not be allowed to take over, however. Often, people want to be able to discuss an issue, so the technology should be backed-up with access to a person who fully understands the policy. Some large organisations such as the London Ambulance Service have a dedicated staff safety officer dealing with violence issues. Most organisations just need to provide a single point of contact for staff.

Openness and honesty

4.46   There is an apparent preoccupation in our society at the moment with 'spin', largely generated by politicians and the media. Although it doesn't seem to have dawned on these people, by and large the public are not taken in by efforts to put a positive gloss on something that is inherently bad news. The public knows it is being 'conned' and it quickly colours the perception of the people who are doing it, evidenced by the low ratings politicians and journalists achieve in any poll about 'trust'. This should be borne in mind when dealing with the more negative aspects of any policy. As with any effective change or process, it is important to be open and honest and to ensure issues and concerns are aired and addressed.

Reinforcement

4.47   The dust will eventually settle on any launch, no matter how much of an impact it has initially made. Reinforcement of the messages with a second wave of communication needs to be made some weeks later. Checking out how well things are going and paying attention to how the policy is being received can be an effective way of finding out the 'weak spots' which are not being followed and the parts that are having an immediate impact. This can be communicated through a newsletter dedicated to workplace violence issues or an area on the intranet. This also provides a vehicle for showing progress against concerns raised by employees.

External communication

4.48 External communication can be a bit of a minefield, especially for a high profile organisation that the media will take a special interest in. The media will naturally look for a story or a slant and care must be taken that the original good intentions are not skewed to provide an interesting angle – at the expense of the launch. Wherever possible, it is a good idea to utilise individuals or departments who are used to handling journalists and the media when planning considering any external communications in this sensitive subject area.

It is vital to plan proactive publicity initiatives and how to react to media attention – perhaps following a serious incident. Through careful thought and planning the organisation can prepare for the inevitable media attention following an incident and turn this into a positive opportunity.

Planning proactive initiatives

4.49 There are a number of ways an organisation can seek publicity for initiatives they have adopted on workplace violence. Firstly, it important to be clear as to the ultimate goal of the publicity, the groups being targeted and the most effective vehicle for achieving it. Some initiatives have done little more than seek a sympathy vote over the terrible problems staff face, and this has reinforced their vulnerability. A more effective deterrent would be to publicise a firm stance against violence being introduced and the success of new security measures and prosecutions.

At the same time it is important to give a strong and unequivocal message to the likely offenders, without alienating the vast numbers of clients, service users and members of the public who wouldn't dream of engaging in abuse or violence towards staff. It is also important to ensure that the action, sanctions and repercussions being advocated are realistic and will happen. It is easy to claim a 'zero tolerance' approach, but these words must be capable of being put into practice or the campaign will lack the hoped for credibility. It is important to ensure that the internal messages are consistent with the external messages.

Media channels

4.50 Nowadays, there is an endless choice of ways to get a message out to service users and members of the public. So much so that it may be advisable to get professional help to target this effectively. Listed below are some of the main ways of getting a message across:

- Newspaper and magazine articles.
- TV/ radio news and documentary programmes.

- Press and TV and radio advertising.

- Leaflet and poster campaigns.

- Website and internet.

Generally, it is possible to retain more 'control' over the content of a message in pre-planned campaigns involving editorial, adverts, posters, leaflets and the like. It becomes more difficult when use is made of the more 'instant' media like press and TV news, and documentaries where it is easy to lose control of the message. Responsible journalists won't try to 'trick' anyone but they do want a newsworthy story and may look for any weakness in the campaign or the opposite point of view from the one being promoted. It may be possible to secure a higher degree of control over magazine or journal articles by securing agreement to review articles before they are published.

Before an interview, it is important to identify what angle the interviewer will be coming from so that the interviewee is prepared to deal with the issues raised; in most circumstances they will be happy to discuss this. It is also vital that prior to any interview the interviewee is clear as to the key messages – a maximum of three – that they will be determined to put across.

Employees likely to be involved in contact with the media should receive specialist training. This also applies to those who may have to attend difficult public meetings such as councillors, planners and corporate spokespersons. These can be extremely challenging and threatening occasions and costly if handled badly.

Media – incident plan

4.51   The current media interest in violence at work can be useful, but if an organisation is not prepared for media attention prior to the 'incident' it may well come out of it somewhat 'battered' by the experience. Adverse publicity can destroy organisations and it is often said that the crisis does not really begin until the media becomes involved. Another consideration is the protection of staff from potentially distressing media 'harassment' and from confidential information getting into the wrong hands, such as personal details including phone numbers and home addresses.

However, with careful preparation, media interest can provide an organisation with a positive public relations opportunity – it is 'on stage' and can either impress or disappoint. Following an incident, emotions will be running high, and pressure will be on managers dealing with it. A clear policy and plan needs to be in existence before it occurs.

In cases that are very serious, perhaps a hostage, kidnap or firearms incident, this can become highly problematic. Crisis management and the media is a highly specialised field in which very few PR and marketing companies have expertise. It is a good idea to seek advice from consultants who specialise in this area if the organisation might be at risk from this type of incident.

New systems, procedures, practices and equipment

4.52 The implementation of a policy will involve the introduction of new systems of working, new procedures, practices and, perhaps, equipment, to learn about and to follow or use. It is essential to develop a plan to introduce and train people in all these areas.

CHAPTER 7 is dedicated to the whole area of training and deals in depth with everything from the initial Training Needs Analysis through to delivery and evaluation of the training.

Implementing the policy

4.53 If the organisation has developed an effective strategy and plan, the actual implementation should be relatively straightforward. Consideration needs to be given to the implications around timing and the extent of training that is required, coupled with the key messages to be emphasised from the beginning.

If there is a long-term training plan because a lot of training has to be achieved it has to be decided who gets what training and when. It makes sense, for example, to train the more vulnerable roles first. It also makes sense to train all new personnel as part of their induction into the organisation.

Once the organisation has identified the need to train people in conflict avoidance and reduction, it is still vulnerable whilst employees undertake their roles whilst still untrained. This is difficult to resolve as it would be unrealistic to close down the operation whilst those people become trained. However, would someone be allowed to work with dangerous chemicals without the appropriate safety equipment?

It is important to be able to establish what training is mandatory based upon the risks faced by staff and that which is simply 'desirable'. Where a significant need for mandatory training has been identified it is important to prioritise this so that the higher risk groups/ areas receive training without delay. Where other staff may have to wait for the full training programme, measures need to be taken to manage risk in the meantime – through, for example, inductions and briefings on key aspects of policy and procedure.

To safeguard the organisation, it is necessary to show a training and development plan that clearly outlines the phases of training being undertaken and the thinking that has gone into the development of those phases and the sequence of training for different roles. There are no 'templates' for this – the organisation should simply be able to evidence why it has decided to approach it in the way that it has.

Evaluating the policy

4.54   It is tempting to feel that the job is done once the policy is in place and the measures are implemented. Certainly the main part of the work has been done, but it is important to test and monitor the reality of whether the policy works in the working environment. It is very likely that polices and practices which made perfect sense in theory will run into trouble when applied in the workplace. It is important, therefore, to monitor and evaluate the implementation of the policy. Evaluation should be undertaken at two levels.

In the short term, there should be proactive testing of the practical implications of the policy. It is a good idea to be aware of areas of the policy that might be untried, sensitive or difficult to implement, and monitor for incidents that test out the practical implications. Affected personnel should be interviewed and feedback obtained which will inform specifically about the policy issues involved. Information from this needs to be analysed and any policy changes made or clarification required should be communicated as quickly as possible.

In the short and longer term, a system needs to be introduced to monitor all incidents of work-related violence which will provide information about the effectiveness of policy, procedures, practices, equipment and training. This will involve a comprehensive reporting and recording process, which is dealt with in CHAPTER 5. It will also involve an effective training evaluation process, which is outlined fully in CHAPTER 7. Both should feed into the overall process for monitoring and evaluating the policy. Figure 4.4 (below) shows a generic model for monitoring a policy.

In this model there are two feedback loops.

1.   An 'immediate loop' where the quality of the measure is evaluated when first received. This will include information about the initial perceptions of the staff about quality of the training, or the usefulness of the equipment, or the workability of a particular policy or procedure. Ideally, this will be sought from the staff, although it will also include unsolicited feedback.

2.   The second feedback loop is through the reporting and recording procedure and the quality of this will be defined by the quality of the information and the information gathering techniques. A well-designed system will provide a wealth of informative data that will ensure the policy is effective.

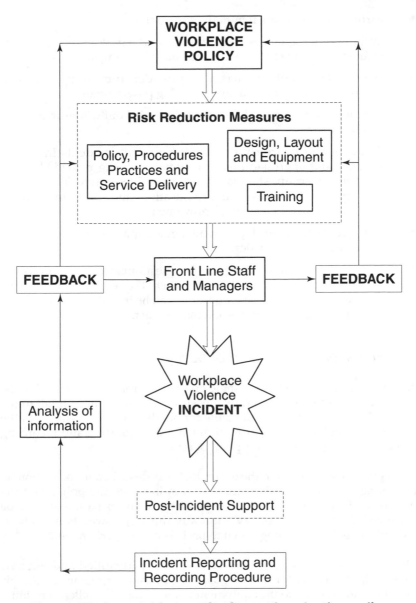

Figure 4.4: A model for monitoring and evaluating policy

The detail of installing such a system will, again, depend very much on the structure, technology and culture of the organisation.

A range of monitoring methods can be used in addition to the recording process. It may be that different methods are suitable for different aspects of the whole staff safety initiative. Here are some ideas:

- Participating in national initiatives or audits.

- Inviting other agencies to be part of staff safety working groups where they are likely to be involved on an inter-agency basis.

- Having the training manager or provider 'dip sample' incident report forms to measure against training programmes.

- Having post-incident risk assessments carried out where an incident involves injury.

- Production of quarterly reports covering all incidents involving violence and aggression with information being provided to the practitioner group, staff safety group and executive. This should identify trends across the organisation and provide possible solutions to areas in need of improvement.

- Setting objectives for departments, geographical areas or teams in terms of violence reduction.

- Introduction of an exit interview or questionnaire – for completion when a staff member leaves either the department or the organisation itself. Specific questions can be introduced to cover the issue of violence and aggression management.

Co-ordination and revision of policy

4.55   It is advisable to have a single point of reference for monitoring the effectiveness of the policy and its measures. Usually, this will fall to the role of the person who is responsible for heath and safety issues. All the immediate feedback and information from the reporting and recording process should go through this point of reference.

It is a good idea to maintain the group that was described in the section on designing the policy, as they are very familiar with the policy and the intention of the various components within it. Information should be reviewed as often as necessary – initially this might well be weekly or monthly, eventually settling down to probably a quarterly review.

The problems and issues should be specifically identified and referred back to the originator for further guidance, revision or replacement. This might include referral to the equipment manufacturer, installer or training provider.

Summary

4.56

Checklist

❏   Full internal or external review of existing situation completed?

❏   Creation of 'policy development group'?

❏   Policy document designed and approved?

❏   Written implementation strategy in place with detailed project plan?

❏   Evaluation and policy review process in place?

---

5 Risk Assessment and Reporting

Introduction

5.1 Risk assessment is at the heart of an effective response to the issues of workplace violence. The key aspects of legislation relating to health and safety issues are explored in **CHAPTER 2**, along with the requirement to undertake an assessment of the risks of violence, just as one would with any other risk.

Once the potential risks have been recognised within an organisation, the next stage is to identify the specific risks associated with each role and then provide measures that will eliminate or minimise the risks identified. Because of its unique and distinct nature, it is important to approach risk assessment for workplace violence separately from that of other common risks. In some areas of work that demand physical intervention training, it is important to consider lifting and handling issues. In the first part of this chapter, the risk assessment process will be examined and will provide a practical approach to assessing the risk of violence to staff throughout an organisation.

The second part of the chapter will look at the reporting and recording process that underpins an effective approach to managing the problems of workplace violence. It will provide advice and guidance about developing a system which suits an organisation together with examples of best practice.

Assessing the risk of workplace violence

5.2 There are three basic ways in which risk of violence can be assessed:

1. Generic violence risk assessment of role.

2. Risk assessment of pre-planned event.

3. Dynamic Risk Assessment.

Generic violence risk assessment of role

5.3 This is, perhaps, the most recognised form of risk assessment. It involves an analysis of all the activities commonly associated with each job role that carries a level of risk from work-related violence. Each activity is examined, the possible risks are identified, and a judgement is made about the likelihood of the perceived risk and the severity of the consequences. Measures to eliminate, minimise or control the risk are then examined and the most appropriate solutions are put into place. These measures should then exist for every person who carries out that role. A good example to illustrate the point is any role that has an element of working alone and visiting clients or service users in their homes.

Some of the risks inherent in such a role are:

- Being targeted by criminals when travelling and in car parks, isolated locations, entrances to flats and apartments.

- Violence from a service user or other individual inside the person's home.

- Being held against will in premises.

- Being injured in an isolated location without access to help.

These risks can increase in high crime areas, when visits are likely to be unwelcome or bring 'bad news', and where the service user is particularly challenging or prone to violence. Measures to eliminate, minimise or control could include:

- Procedures in relation to callout, providing details of location, client visits, times of appointments to a central source and call in when complete.

- Personal safety guidance to reduce vulnerability when travelling and visiting.

- Training in Dynamic Risk Assessment, conflict resolution, communication skills etc.

- Provision of equipment where appropriate such as a mobile phone or attack alarm.

- Paired working when there is a greater risk of violence – associated for example with the service user, location, time or nature of visit.

Each role should be examined in this way to determine all the risks and measures appropriate for that role.

Once this assessment and the resulting control measures have been established for a role, then everyone performing that role should be required to have the appropriate equipment, conform to the procedures and undertake the training required.

Management should ensure that the generic violence risk assessment is carried out on all roles where there is a potential danger and that the control measures are clearly stated and understood by everyone in each role.

Violence risk assessment – pre-planned event

5.4   The generic violence risk assessment caters well for the main activities of a role. However, in every job there are events and activities that are out of the ordinary or, perhaps, done only rarely. It is quite possible that the generic risk assessment will not cover every circumstance and, in such cases, it is important to assess the risk involved in an event or activity as part of the planning process. For example, a licensing enforcement role in a council involves lone working and visiting premises. This is catered for in the generic risk assessment for the role. Occasionally, the post holder may have to carry out observations on licensed premises to gather information about late drinking and other infringements. This is a pre-planned event and a risk assessment should be done on the planned operation. This will include issues specific to this event such as time of day, type of location, method of observation, and the type of groups expected around the area. The risk assessment will identify if there is an increased risk of potential for violence and a need for extra measures in these circumstances. This might include not carrying out the event if the risks cannot be effectively managed. In this example the risks could be reduced by:

- Ensuring that at least two people are involved in the event.

- Carrying out observations discreetly at a safe distance and out of the view of the general public.

- Ensuring that those involved have received appropriate training.

- Ensuring that those involved have the ability to summon assistance if necessary.

- Informing the police of the activity where this is appropriate.

The risk assessment should be recorded and included in the planning documentation for the event itself. A simple form and checklist can be developed for such pre-planned events.

Dynamic Risk Assessment

5.5   There are many occasions when front line staff are confronted with situations which are unique and not catered for in a generic risk assessment or assessment of a planned event. These are often the situations where people get hurt because they don't have a way of assessing the risks in the situation they are confronted with, and do not respond appropriately.

Maybo, as a conflict specialist, has developed a 'Dynamic Risk Assessment' process which helps an individual to effectively assess a situation from a personal safety perspective, as it is unfolding. The person can continuously assess the circumstances and adjust his or her response to meet the risk presented moment by moment. One of the greatest threats to an individual is complacency. This is something that anyone can fall prey to and often happens because the individual concerned has performed a task hundreds of times before. Being approached by a member of the public, finding someone asleep in a waiting area or departure lounge, visiting premises – all are part of the routine of a job and it is easy to miss if there are no obvious signs of danger.

The Maybo model is called 'SAFER' and it serves to increase peoples' awareness of the risks that they are facing in any particular situation. It helps them to evaluate the situation and respond in the most effective way.

- S = Step back

- A = Assess threat

- F = Find help

- E = Evaluate options

- R = Respond

Step back

5.6   The moment a threatening incident occurs people instinctively prepare themselves mentally and physically. This is known as the 'fight or flight' response. At this point people naturally react emotionally to the situation and find it harder to think clearly and rationally. This results in a tendency to either rush in, or be sucked in, to a situation and this radically reduces a person's ability to be fully effective.

- Don't rush in – even to help someone else.

- Physically step back, if possible – more can be seen and there is a better chance of assessing the individual/ situation correctly.

- Mentally and emotionally step back – think clearly and rationally.

Assess threat

5.7   This involves identifying the potential dangers and level of threat by using a second model 'POP' (see **5.11–5.13** below).

Find help

5.8   Consider what help is needed, or who can be communicated with. Invariably help is often called too late, when events have already gone out of control. Seeking help early enough can assist significantly in the ability to cope and deal with an incident rationally. The scale of help needed will depend on the issue, the situation and the behaviour of all concerned.

- Consider calling the police or security for assistance.

- Seek help from people nearby.

- Ask a manager or other colleagues to take over (switching).

- Request a manager or other colleague to watch – either to call for more help, or to assist directly.

- Consider getting a colleague to telephone back later to check that the individual concerned is okay.

Evaluate options

5.9   This involves deciding what options are available and selecting the ones most likely to work. There are generally three main options:

- To exit.

   The emotional reaction to incidents can result in individuals not breaking away from an incident or not leaving early enough. This can exacerbate the situation or put the person at greater risk.

- To pass control of the incident to another.

- To deal with the person, rationally selecting an appropriate approach.

Response

5.10   The individual should respond by using the best course of action – which may be to leave. Throughout the response the threat, the ability to behave and think rationally, and the effectiveness of the strategy, needs to be continually assessed.

The situation should be continually assessed using SAFER.

The 'POP' model is also very useful in helping people consciously assess the risks presented in a situation. It is very simple and can be performed within a few moments or completed over some time whilst watching an event unfold. It will also provide a useful framework when explaining ones actions at a later date.

Person

5.11   What is it about a person that causes them to be perceived as a threat? Staff should continually assess people to judge whether there is a risk to others or themselves. Essentially this requires careful examination of the behaviour and body language of customers, patients and service users to spot the warning signs at the earliest opportunity eg:

- What is their history? Have they been violent before?

- Have they had a bad experience with the organisation, today or some time preceding?

- Are they impaired through drink or drugs?

- Do they have an advantage in terms of size, strength and fitness? (Great care should be taken not to eliminate a risk if a person is smaller, older or apparently infirm. For example in one reported incident a health visitor on a home visit to an elderly bed-ridden patient was grabbed by the hair and repeatedly hit against the side of the bed.)

- Are other people present likely to support you or the other person should they become violent?

It is worth noting that when reviewing events after an incident a common staff comment is that they had felt uncomfortable or knew there would be a problem the moment they saw the individual. Sadly, although the 'mental radar' picks up the key signals subconsciously, this does not automatically lead to a conscious decision to leave the situation. By being more pro-active in identifying the state of an individual, and adjusting their own behaviour and actions as appropriate, staff can radically improve personal safety. Some key points to watch out for are:

- Eye contact – too strong or too little.*

- Invasion of personal space.*

- Hunched or tensed shoulders and upper body.

- Vocal – overly loud or very quiet and no preamble in first communication, such as 'good morning'.

* Consider these points in the context of possible cultural differences.

Object

5.12 The risk from objects either present, or in the possession of the aggressor need to be considered.

They may include:

- Moving vehicles

  For example, an irate driver having been given a ticket for breaching parking legislation might get into their car and drive at the parking attendant in a fit of anger.

- Knives and other edged or blunt weapons

  If the person's hands are concealed be aware that they may have a weapon.

- Apparently innocent articles such as syringes, DIY tools, and bottles or beer cans

  For example in one reported incident a teacher was attacked by an aggressive pupil. The child grabbed a pencil and lunged at the teacher. The pencil was stabbed into the teacher's hand. A second example involved a nurse who left her hospital and was accosted at the gate by an old man on crutches. The man struck the nurse with the crutch.

Place

5.13　The location can present different threats depending on the time of day or night, lighting conditions and the absence of any escape routes. A key element to the Dynamic Risk Assessment is the continual knowledge of where exits are as well as ensuring the careful positioning and availability of escape routes if needed.

Environment issues that may have to be considered include:

- Is the location a remote area away from the observation of others or a safe refuge?

- The routes available to and from work.

- Does interaction take place in a limited number of areas?

- Are there any exits that are blocked?

Consideration should be given to the way that staff are positioned in rooms. Staff should position themselves in order to be able to see and use exits if the need should arise. Such positioning should ensure that the aggressor is, wherever possible, able to see and use the exits as well. After all, if staff 'block' the exit by standing in front of it, an aggressor's 'fight or flight' reaction has had the flight removed, leaving a dangerous option. Such considerations can impact on interview and reception area design.

Risk assessment – who and how?

Who should do it?

5.14　There is little doubt that the individual who is working at the customer interface dealing with conflict and confrontation with the clients, service users and the public on a daily basis, is best placed to be able to identify the risks faced. He or she will also be able to offer the most practical and workable solutions to the risks identified. In fact, there is no doubt that the people in these situations will already be aware of the issues and will also be using strategies on a daily basis to deal with the problems.

There are some down sides to this. Sometimes it is difficult to see the wood for the trees. Being so close to such situations can desensitise people and lead to complacency about the dangers or about the individual's ability to deal with the perceived risks. It is particularly easy to miss the dangers in things that are done regularly and without any apparent difficulty. Evolved ways of fulfilling the role can bring with it some downsides.

In a culture where staff accept workplace violence as 'just part of the job', and where little training and supervision is provided on how to deal with such issues, leading to the belief that a dangerous workplace is normal – can result in staff being less able to objectively see the risks. For example, planning regulation enforcers from a central London local authority declared that they often recognise the danger of entering particular properties on their own. However, in practice they perceived it as 'part of the job' and no protective measures were put in place. In other words, they saw the potential danger but were conditioned into accepting it as a norm.

All this can make it difficult for someone who is doing the role every day to undertake a comprehensive risk assessment of his or her role. The Maybo Dynamic Risk Assessment model is designed to address this in 'live' situations where the individual needs to be able to identify these risks 'on their feet' and quickly choose the most effective solutions.

For generic violence risk assessment of roles, the process needs to include someone who is trained and experienced in identifying risks and who can spot the hidden dangers in workplace environments, situations and incidents where risks exist but are not obvious. The most effective solution is to combine the two – a person who is trained in risk assessment and has experience in the management of violence, should examine the roles alongside the people who carry out those roles on a day-to-day basis.

For pre-planned events, people who understand the roles involved should plan the event itself and then work with someone who understands risk assessment to identify the possible risks and appropriate solutions.

Most organisations see the line manager as an important element and train them in understanding the skills required to undertake a risk assessment. In practice, it is very likely that most organisations will already have a number of people who are trained in risk assessment for general health and safety issues. The methodology and techniques are the same, only the context is different. It is a relatively straightforward task to develop their existing skills to include risk assessment of workplace violence. It is important however that they possess a good understanding of violence at work and how it can be controlled.

It is a good idea to consider working alongside an outside consultant with specialist knowledge on violence, to help with the development of violence risk assessment processes and control measures. As an outsider, they can see things more objectively. They are able to ask the difficult questions and challenge the status quo. They will also bring a good deal of experience in the field of work-related violence and, if they have worked with other organisations in a particular sector, can quickly provide effective and proven solutions to the problems. Organisations that provide personal safety type training will not always have expertise on these wider management issues, so be sure to select genuine specialists.

How should it be approached?

5.15   As always, the approach used will depend very much on the organisation, its structure, culture and general approach to health and safety issues. If an approach to risk assessment of health and safety in the workplace already exists it should not be too difficult to adapt it for the specialised task of risk assessment for workplace violence. Perhaps the biggest difference is to approach the assessment on a role-specific basis rather than purely on a geographical area or departmental basis.

By definition, the risk of workplace violence will always involve some sort of interaction with another person. This is a unique feature and has an impact upon how risk assessments should be approached. In risk assessments for the majority of the areas of health and safety, the risks are passive – waiting for the unwary to trip, fall, spill etc. In many cases, attention to safety equipment, safe-use procedures etc will offer a reasonable guarantee that if precautions are taken the risk will be minimised.

The risks of work-related violence are much more difficult to predict and to control because it is hard to predict the range of responses that someone might use in a situation involving conflict. The use of protective equipment, for example, has drawbacks in this area. If someone is welding, then wearing protective gloves and goggles is done as a matter of course and no one would think twice about it. It would however be unrealistic, and possibly counterproductive, to expect all workers that face a risk of violence to wear stab-proof vests. The image and psychological message created would be disproportionate to the risk involved in all but the most hazardous roles.

The most important focus in assessing the risks of work-related violence is the actual role being undertaken. For each role the following main areas need to be assessed:

●   What contact is made with the clients, patients, service users or members of the public? This will usually be described in the job description. For example, enforcing role, caring profession, advising or dealing with complaints.

- What sort of people generally make up this contact? For example, travelling public, offenders, patients, clients or relatives.

- Where does the contact take place? For example, interview rooms, reception, platform, home address, classroom or on the streets.

- What sort of 'state' will the client/ patient etc be in? For example, will they be influenced by drink or drugs, anxious, frustrated or hostile?

- What specific tasks are performed? For example, handling complaints, delivering 'bad news', denying benefits, evicting, arresting, or even treating an individual.

Content of the risk assessment

5.16 The risk assessment itself should be a 'live' document that provides an up to date summary of the risks of violence associated with a particular role. Each role should be examined to identify the potential risk of workplace-related violence that exists for someone performing that role. The first question to be asked is: 'Is there any likelihood that someone doing this role will be abused, threatened or assaulted in circumstances relating to their work?'

If the answer is 'yes', then a risk assessment for workplace violence needs to be carried out.

Figure 5.1 (below) outlines five steps that provide a basic risk assessment model for both the generic risk assessment and for the risk assessment of a pre-planned event.

Step 1 – Identify the risks inherent in the role and plan consultation

5.17 A good job description provides an excellent starting point for identifying risks associated with a specific role. An examination should show the potential situations where the jobholder will be at risk. This will be obvious in many cases if the role involves duties like enforcement, dealing with complaints or people who are under the influence of drink or drugs. However, this should only be regarded as the starting point. Few job descriptions will capture all the possible scenarios that might arise and other sources of information should be used. This is why at Step 2 and Step 3 of this process workers will be consulted in order to identify the practical situations where risks occur.

At Step 1 it is also important to research other potentially useful sources of information such as HSE and sector-specific guidance/research. It is also worth contacting other local organisations and those in similar areas of

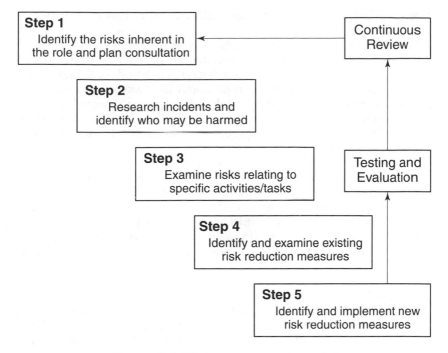

Figure 5.1: Risk assessment model

work. These may offer valuable insight into what to look for, and practical control measures.

Steps 2 and 3 involve consultation with workers and this needs to be planned carefully to ensure this covers a cross section of managers and staff performing the roles being risk assessed, and also those in supporting roles who may add valuable insight. The consultation can take the form of a combination of the following:

- Structured and informal interviews.

- Small focus groups (typically 3–6 staff).

- Questionnaires.

- Workplace observation.

It is important to co-ordinate visits in advance and agree the plan with local management and staff representatives. If this process is done well, there is a better chance that staff 'buy in' to it and embrace subsequent risk reduction measures and training. Visits to work areas should be undertaken at different times to ensure that observations reflect the situation at night for example (where shifts and out of hours working operate).

Step 2 – Research incidents and identify who may be harmed

5.18 An examination and analysis of past-incident reports, local log books etc associated with workplace violence will provide invaluable data in a risk assessment. Ideally, an effective reporting and recording system will provide continuous information about the risks associated with a particular role. Unfortunately violence is under-reported in most organisations so it is important to try to establish the true extent of the problem by consulting with managers and staff, and gathering anecdotal evidence of occurrences.

The priority will be to identify risks to the jobholder. However, there is a duty of care towards anyone who might be harmed in violent incidents and therefore the assessment should extend to include any individuals who may be involved in the contact, eg regular staff, contractors, security staff, other patients or service users, caretakers, porters, members of the public and temporary staff. This should also consider the aggressor as well.

The consultation should therefore extend to some of these groups for example, speak to the receptionists, caretakers and security staff. Logs kept by these groups may also provide useful information on incidents, and these people will add valuable insight to the problems experienced.

Step 3 – Examine risks relating to the specific activities and tasks performed

5.19 Assessing the level of risk has its difficulties. Some roles, by their very nature, have a risk of violence almost 'built in'. This is particularly true of a role involving enforcement such as a traffic warden. Other roles have a high level of customer contact, a receptionist for example, but a low level of potential conflict. By reviewing the actual activities and tasks performed it is possible to get a realistic measure of the risks involved and to ensure controls are both relevant and proportionate.

This stage involves in depth consultation and problem solving with managers and workers, with a view to establishing:

• The risks associated with specific activities and tasks performed

  Risk activities and tasks could include travel and home visits, delivering bad news, cash handling, confronting trespassers or fare evaders, or giving certain treatments. The risks may be compounded at certain times and locations, or by factors relating to service users or other persons who may, for example, present challenging behaviour, be influenced by drink or drugs, or, have a history of crime and/ or violence.

• Practical risk reduction and support measures

Those performing the job will often have the best ideas for reducing risk and it is important that the underlying causes of conflict and possible solutions are identified. This will also help to ensure that controls put in place are workable and likely to be adopted by staff. Whilst consulting workers, take the opportunity to explore any formal or informal risk reduction measures that have been adopted to date, and consider their opinions on the effectiveness of them (this information will be valuable at Step 4).

When considering the risks present in job activities and tasks, it is helpful to identify the risk level based on two elements:

1. the *likelihood* of harm actually being caused, and

2. the likely impact or *severity* of the harm caused.

The *likelihood* can be assessed on a sliding scale such as:

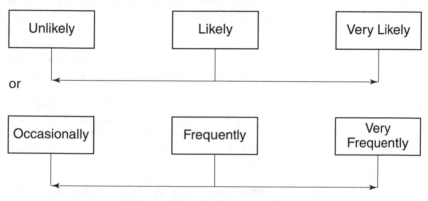

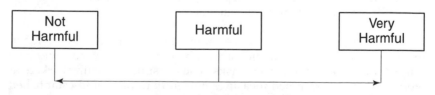

Figure 5.2: Likelihood of harm

The *severity* of harm can be assessed on a similar scale such as:

Figure 5.3: Severity of harm

From this, a 'risk rating' can be established which identifies the risk as being low, medium or high. When considering the impact/ severity of an incident there a number of considerations including:

- Physical harm to those involved.

- Emotional impact on staff.

- Impact on the perpetrator and other service users.

- Numbers of people involved.

- Duration of the incident.

- Effect on operations and service delivery.

- Financial impact on both individuals and organisation.

The likelihood/ impact approach to risk assessment is long established and is helpful in providing a broad assessment of risk. However, used on its own it can be somewhat 'pseudo-scientific' – apparently providing a neat and effective answer to the problem when, in fact, it only provides part of the picture. For example, it does not take into account the fear of violence experienced by the person doing the job. The actual occurrence of ambulance crews being stabbed may be very low statistically. However, the impact/ severity of such an assault would be extremely high and one can understand staff fears. An employer has a duty to include this in the risk assessment and respond to this fear, for example through rationalising fears in training and introducing guidance to further minimise the risk.

It is also easy to underestimate the impact on staff of continuous low-level verbal abuse and intimidation. This can lead to stress-related illness and affect for example, staff working in reception areas or call centres, who may not at first appear to be at risk.

Step 4 – Identify and examine existing risk reduction measures

5.20   There will be existing risk reduction measures already in place. These may be there formally through an earlier risk assessment by the employer or introduced informally by the staff who have recognised the risk and decided to do something about it. There may be informal procedures like calling in before going off duty or working in pairs in particular areas or with particular clients.

These existing measures need to be compared with the risks identified in the assessment and an evaluation made about their effectiveness and how relative they are to the current risks. The consultation with workers at Step 3 will have examined measures currently in place and established what has worked for them and what has not.

Step 5 – Identify and implement new risk reduction measures

5.21   Effective measures for reducing the assessed risks should be identified and implemented. At Step 2 and Step 3 of this risk assessment process good ideas will have been gathered on risk reduction through consultation with workers. These may be a combination of safer working practices and procedures, policy, training and equipment. Risk reduction measures are examined further in CHAPTER 6.

The solution needs to take into account all the factors including an evaluation of the cost of risk reduction measures relative to the risk itself. Some measures have serious cost implications. Having staff working in pairs, could for example, enhance productivity in some roles as the result of increased confidence, or equally reduce productivity if they work ineffectively. Equally important is the impact of the measures. Is the provision of a safety glass screen the most effective way of protecting staff from abuse or is it likely to further distance and frustrate service users and increase conflict? It will be easier to prioritise and focus resources if at Step 3 the potential risks have been graded in terms of likelihood and severity.

Risk assessment forms

5.22 It is important that risk assessment for violence should be consistent across all roles and it is common practice to devise and use a specifically designed form for this process. Some caution is needed here. Forms can quite easily become a fixed process and lead to a single-minded approach – 'if there isn't a box for it it's not important.' In reality, there can be an infinite number of situations where there is a potential for conflict and violence, and some of the most dangerous may be the least obvious.

For this reason, an 'example' form has not been provided here. A risk assessment form should be designed to meet the specific needs of the specific organisation. The main principle is to follow the steps outlined in the model and the form should be designed to facilitate that process, whilst allowing the person carrying out the assessment to think 'outside the boxes'.

Continuous review

5.23 The risk assessment for each role should be a 'live' document. Staff should have easy access to it and should be encouraged to involve themselves in the process of keeping the assessment live and up to date.

Reports of incidents involving violence should be collated and analysed to provide data and information that will keep the risk assessment for each role up to date. This will be the substance of the remainder of this chapter and a model for an effective reporting and recording process will be provided.

Summary

5.24

Checklist

Workplace violence risk assessments

❑   Specific risk assessments for workplace violence.

❑   Assessments made on each role performed, including:

  - What client contact occurs?

  - What types of people are involved?

  - What state people are in?

  - Where and when contact is made?

  - What specific activities and tasks are performed?

❑   Assessment completed by, or in conjunction with, health and safety officer, trained line manager and/ or external consultant.

❑   Staff must be involved and informed.

❑   Content to include:

  - Identification of inherent risks and plan for consultation.

  - Research of incidents and identification of who may be harmed.

  - Specific risk activities and tasks performed.

  - Existing risk reduction measures.

  - New risk reduction measures.

❑   Risk assessments to be monitored and reviewed regularly.

❑   Additional assessments:

  - For pre-planned events – incorporated in event planning process.

  - Dynamic Risk Assessment – personal process to assess interactions.

Reporting, recording and monitoring system

5.25   Central to an effective strategy for combating workplace violence is an understanding of the nature and extent of the problem. Integral to this is a system that monitors and provides data and information about the trends surrounding violence in the workplace for a particular organisation.

There are a number of benefits that accrue from the introduction of a well designed system that provides for effective reporting, recording and monitoring of incidents of work-related violence, including:

- The wealth of information gathered can provide evidence on the strengths or weaknesses of risk reduction measures such as policies, procedures, management skills, equipment, training and selection and service provision.

- The details offered from a reporting system provide a solid foundation for the risk assessment process, policy development and overall workplace violence strategy.

- Reporting on workplace violence is an essential base of data from which to check, test and improve health and safety and service delivery policies and procedures.

- Establish hot spots, environmental issues, staff issues and customer processes that may be contributing to customer aggression.

- The reporting process can be a trigger for staff care and communication, particularly when they are most vulnerable.

- Training issues can be identified on an individual basis or a wider organisational front and reports can indicate where staff need further training.

- A sound reporting process can also provide a wealth of scenarios and situations to base realistic training on. This ensures that training is relevant and has the best potential for preparing staff in dealing with extremely difficult people issues.

Figure 5.4 (below) shows a typical model of an effective reporting and monitoring system for workplace violence and the rest of this chapter will concentrate upon developing a practical solution based upon it.

Designing the system

5.26 The design of an effective system should be comprehensive – but not over complicated. It is important to get it right from the start and help should be sought from an individual or department that is experienced in developing such systems. It may be worth investing in outside consultants who specialise in this area.

As with any system, the most important and difficult task is to think carefully about the precise outcomes required from a reporting and recording system.

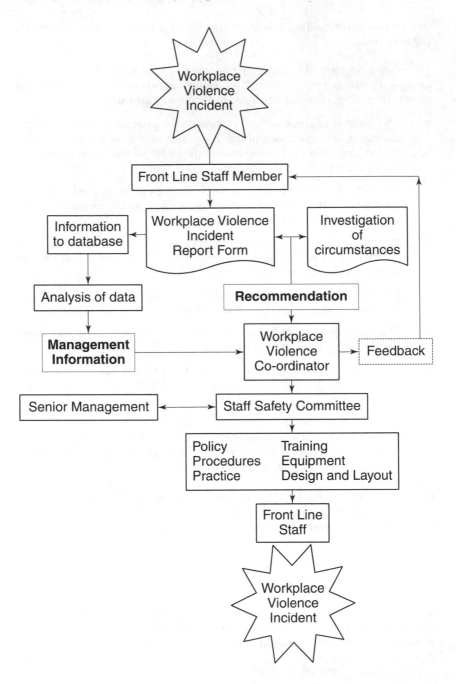

Workplace
Violence
Incident

Front Line Staff Member

Information
to database

Workplace Violence
Incident
Report Form

Investigation
of
circumstances

Analysis of data

Recommendation

**Management
Information**

Workplace
Violence
Co-ordinator

Feedback

Senior Management

Staff Safety Committee

Policy
Procedures
Practice

Training
Equipment
Design and Layout

Front Line
Staff

Workplace
Violence
Incident

**Figure 5.4: A model for reporting and monitoring incidents of
workplace violence**

These outcomes will be specific to the needs of a particular organisation and are likely to include:

- Information which will provide immediate and direct feedback about potentially harmful or dangerous circumstances which need to be addressed urgently.

- An investigation process which will examine the circumstances of an incident and provide recommendations for clarifying, fine tuning or improving policy, procedure, practice, design and layout, training and equipment.

- A database which will record comprehensive details of each incident of workplace violence within the organisation.

- A process of analysis, which will provide detailed management information about the incidence of workplace violence across the organisation. This information can be used to inform policy, procedure, practice, design and layout, equipment and training.

- A communication and monitoring process which will ensure the relevant information is identified and gets to the right people and departments.

To achieve these outcomes, the essential elements are:

- A dedicated workplace violence incident report form.

- An investigation process (and training in its application).

- An information database and analysis process.

- A workplace violence co-ordinator.

- A communication process.

Workplace violence incident report form

5.27   The design of the form will depend on many factors, some of which will be dictated by the way that the information is to be recorded and analysed. Nowadays, it is almost certain that a computer will be used to analyse the data and provide the appropriate management information and this will influence the way that the form is designed.

One important principle is the 'user-friendly' nature of the form. Most organisations suffer from chronic under-reporting in this area and some of this is undoubtedly down to the ease, or otherwise, with which the report is completed. The organisational desire to use one form for all accidents and occurrences can result in intimidating forms, designed to satisfy the needs of a hungry computer database. This can be at the expense of the needs of someone who has been through a harrowing incident and has to complete the form before he or she can go home. The rule needs to be – keep it simple and keep it short, and specific to violence.

The following details are suggested as a minimum whether using a dedicated violence report, or a combined use report form:

● Name and contact details of the person making the report.

● Date, time and location of incident.

● Description of the incident and any injuries sustained.

● Details of any other staff involved.

● Details of the assailant.

● Details of any possible witnesses.

Further information will be required from the incident form, but this will differ between organisations based upon the management data required. The section that follows below on 'measurable outcomes' (see **5.38**) gives an indication as to some of the additional information a dedicated report form can capture.

Where possible, it helps to present people with questions to which they can tick an appropriate box. This has an additional benefit in that it can be coded into a computer very easily. However, an important part of this form is the victim's account of the incident and this should be a written narrative of the events. If it is completed as soon as possible after the incident it could then serve as an original note which the victim may be able to refer to in any subsequent legal proceedings.

The report form can also provide the basis for recording post-incident action by the line manager, including staff support, the investigation process and subsequent recommendations and actions.

The investigation process

5.28   It is important that the circumstances of the incident are properly investigated so that the facts surrounding it can be established and everyone can learn from it. It is equally important that the staff member who is the victim of the incident does not feel that he or she is being blamed for what happened. The member of staff may have failed to follow a procedure or had an unhelpful attitude but nothing gives a client, service user or member of the public the right to abuse threaten or physically assault that member of staff. It is all too easy for the report to conclude that: 'if the member of staff had followed the policy, the assault would not have happened'.

The point here is that the investigation process should intend to establish the facts of the incident and make recommendations that will help to reduce the risk of this type of incident happening again. There may, of course, be individual development needs for the victim, for example to help them to manage similar situations in the future. Although people have different conflict management styles, few actually relish the idea of being abused, threatened or assaulted or actively invite such consequences. It might be worth exploring the reasons why the individual failed to follow policy or procedure. It may be that this is not clear or is difficult to implement in practice.

In most organisations, the person who carries out the investigation will be a manager, probably of the victim of the incident. It is worth considering whether, in fact, this needs to be the case. In a large organisation, for example, it could part of the role of a properly trained person who is not part of the management function.

The recommendations from this investigation will be fed directly to the person responsible for co-ordinating issues of workplace violence for a decision as to how they should be taken forward. Some information might need to be fed quickly into the organisation if a particular risk is identified and is ongoing. Some may need to be fed into policy and procedure for a change in practice or to the training department for changes to training.

Information database and analysis

5.29 The information gathered from all the incidents of workplace violence can provide an invaluable insight into the trends, hotspots and risks that are not obvious in the day to day management of such incidents. To make the best use of this information, it is important to develop a flexible database that will allow the maximum manipulation of the stored data. For example, important information can be gained about risks of violence in particular roles by searching across incidents according to periods of time. If there is a statistically significant increase in physical assaults to staff between 9 pm and 11 pm on Friday and Saturday then risk reduction measures, perhaps working in pairs, can be introduced. Monitoring data on a regular basis, perhaps monthly, will identify trends and risk 'hotspots' which can then be further investigated for cause and appropriate risk reduction measures.

The database also provides a powerful tool for monitoring the effectiveness of risk reduction measures by monitoring over a similar period to see if the measures have impacted upon the identified risks.

Ideally, a purpose-designed database will provide a 'Rolls Royce' in terms of management information. However, a well-designed spreadsheet can offer an adequate substitute and will provide useful information although with less flexibility.

Workplace violence co-ordinator

5.30 It is vitally important, particularly in a large organisation, to have one person who is responsible for the co-ordination of information and recommendations that result from the incident reports. This person (it may, of course, be a department) will be responsible for:

- Maintaining the reporting and recording procedure.

- Monitoring the quality of the content and the investigation process.

- Monitoring the recommendations from the reporting and investigation process.

- Searching and monitoring the database for useful management information, trends, and hotspots that need further investigation.

- Informing the Staff Safety Committee of recommendations and work-related violence issues for discussion and further action.

- Monitoring the effectiveness of risk reduction measures.

- Liaising with the police and other relevant agencies.

- Administering or assisting in the process of litigation or action against the attacker.

The Staff Safety Committee, described in CHAPTER 4, will support this role and its members will provide help across their areas and functions in monitoring and reducing risk.

The London Ambulance Service actually has a full time staff safety officer who co-ordinates key aspects of strategy and also links with the police on issues such as prosecution. A full-time post may not be viable in smaller organisations, but someone still needs to take responsibility for the monitoring and overall co-ordination of a violence strategy, as part of their role.

A communication process

5.31 Any reporting and recording system is only as good as the communication process used to get information to staff. It is not unusual to review an organisation that provides a well written policy on work-place violence and a sophisticated reporting system only to find that few staff are aware of it or understand the process. Quite often polices gather dust on the shelves of managers and the staff fail to report or record the majority of the incidents.

A clear communication process should be built into the system so that the front line staff are kept fully aware of the most up to date policy, procedure and practice for their role. A common complaint is that individuals complete incident forms and then hear nothing more about the outcomes. A feedback loop should be an integral part of the system so that people see that their input is taken seriously and is seen to make a difference.

Implementation

5.32   Even the most sophisticated system in the world is doomed to fail if it is not properly implemented. Most people are sceptical about anything new and need to be convinced of the benefits. The process of change is discussed in CHAPTER 4.

The following five areas are key to successful implementation of a reporting process:

1.   Management involvement and training.

2.   Staff training.

3.   Provision of resources.

4.   Monitoring the completion of reports.

5.   Provision of feedback to those affected and information to the wider organisation.

Manager involvement and training

5.33   Managers at every level need to understand and appreciate the complete reporting, recording and monitoring process. Line managers in particular are key as they will be directly responsible for the incident report forms. Training for managers should be comprehensive and completed in advance of the launch of the new system.

Staff training

5.34   Ultimately the system will rely on staff completing reports properly. Training helps to establish best practice and a sound consistent approach. It ensures that individuals understand the importance of the process and that completion is part of their duty of care. It is also a good opportunity to emphasise the benefits which effective reporting and recording will bring, especially in terms of increased safety. Training works well if it is incorporated into other training for workplace-related violence, making a logical progression from being involved in and dealing with an incident to reporting it.

Provision of resources

5.35   The integrity of a new system can be badly affected by lack of basic resources required and the provision of sufficient forms and guidance is of significant importance. It is easy to overlook satellite offices or remote locations and this can have a strong negative impact on the process.

Monitoring the completion of reports

5.36 The design and initial launch can often be the easy part of implementation. The real test comes as the weeks and months go by. Four fundamental questions need to be asked on a routine basis:

- Are all relevant incidents being recorded?

- Are reports correctly entered?

- Are accounts of incidents adequate and professional?

- Is anything actually being done as a consequence?

Feedback and regular provision of information across the organisation

5.37 Following the introduction of a reporting process, particular effort must be made to provide immediate and ongoing feedback in relation to reported incidents. This applies not only to the affected individual, but across the whole organisation. This can take the form of:

- Personal feedback to staff.

- Indications as to future action.

- Regular updates as to progress including action against offender.

- Regular detailed information fed to affected department and to others with similar problems.

- Monthly briefings at staff meetings.

This is where good line manager training will pay dividends. In the beginning, people will happily fill in reports. As the novelty wears off and they fail to see immediate benefits, the reporting will begin to decline. Line managers need to monitor this and ensure reports are submitted were appropriate. Equally, it is important to continue to feed information back to the front line staff about the improvements that are being achieved. Sharing graphs and charts showing the information being gained, for example, will maintain interest. Newsletters and briefings can highlight trends, safe practice, and action taken as a result of staff feedback.

A *formal review* of the reporting system should be undertaken between six and twelve months after initial implementation. In the main it should seek to establish whether the system is being used, whether it can be improved and what is being done with the information generated.

An essential element in the review is to establish how front line staff view it and what feedback they receive following submission of reports. To fully achieve staff support, they need to feel that the process is not merely an academic exercise, or worse, a process to protect the management.

Measurable outcomes

5.38 A good reporting, recording and monitoring process provides endless opportunity for measuring things and it is tempting to draw lots of conclusions from the statistical data that is available.

Measurable outcomes using information from the reporting process may include:

- The number of injuries to staff.

- The number of injuries to service users.

- The extent and type of injuries suffered.

- The number of working days lost due to assaults on staff.

- The number of prosecutions taken against those assaulting staff.

- Extent to which safety procedures have been followed.

- Which techniques taught in training have been used and their effectiveness.

- Incident and assault patterns.

- The groups at most risk.

- The highest risk tasks and activities.

- Profiles of perpetrators of violence.

The more sophisticated the database, the more comparisons and measures available.

Caution needs to be exercised here, as it is easy to make fundamental mistakes about 'cause' and 'effect'. For example, a laudable goal on the introduction of a policy about work-related violence is to 'reduce the number of work-related incidents by x% over the next 12 months.' In practice, the most common outcome of introducing an effective policy and training in this area is to increase the number of reported incidents. Equally, great store can be invested in a training programme to develop positive attitudes towards violence and aggression in new recruits. It is tempting to make comparisons between these recruits and a sample of existing staff in the same role. Such a comparison assumes training is the only variable and fails to recognise the negative impact, for example, that the existing culture will have upon those recruits when they join the workforce and have to 'fit in' to be accepted.

Under-reporting

5.39 It has been mentioned several times that most organisations suffer from under-reporting of workplace violence-related incidents. The consequences can be far reaching:

In one NHS Trust a review of violence provided a considerable amount of anecdotal evidence from front line staff regarding injuries sustained during endoscopies (specifically an internal examination process placing examination tubes down a patient's throat). Numerous staff had been injured with sprains and bruising as patients lashed out during the uncomfortable procedure. One staff member had been on sick leave for several months for an injury suffered during this process. When the Trust chairman was asked about the problem the response was, 'what problem?' A reporting process was available, but, for a variety of reasons, was not being used to record these incidents of violence. Several issues were identified that were a direct consequence of the incidents; nursing staff morale was suffering, staff turnover and sickness levels were high putting increasing pressure on a stretched service, equipment was being damaged and the Trust was running the risk of a failure of duty of care. The Trust's reporting system would have picked up the 'hotspot' but the incidents were not being reported.

There are a number of reasons why incidents are not reported:

- Failure to fill out the reports. This can be due to several reasons eg laziness of individuals or an organisational culture of not completing administrative elements of the role.

- The feeling of 'pointlessness' – 'why report it as nothing ever changes'. This may well be the perception amongst staff; organisations often do make changes but fail to communicate the message to front line staff or offer feedback to those involved.

- Fear of criticism having brought an incident to light. This is a particular problem in organisations where a culture of blame exists. 'If you had followed the correct procedure you wouldn't have been assaulted.'

- Over complicated and lengthy reporting forms and processes and uncertainty in how to report and account for actions.

- Failure to report low level workplace violence. Staff and managers may perceive verbal abuse and threats as 'an occupational hazard'. This provides a culture of accepting the behaviour and although it may not be practical to put in a report every time someone swears, care must be taken not to underestimate the possible long-term effects of such behaviour. Clearly no person should be expected to go to work to be sworn at, insulted or threatened.

- Failure to recognise some types of incidents as 'workplace violence', particularly unintentional injury from, for example, clinical conditions as outlined in the NHS example above.

Disclosure rules

5.40   It must always be borne in mind that written records of any incident that results in a court case may be called upon as evidence. This would include any internal incident reports, notes, debriefing notes, statements or correspondence. Such material may be held on computer or paper, and CCTV recordings will often be required. This can be a far-reaching requirement drawing from elements not directly linked with the incident itself, for example during a trial of a police officer, a T-shirt was produced in evidence. The clothing had been worn during training by the officer's trainer. It was claimed that the nature of the text on the T-shirt demonstrated a degree of attitude and behaviour, which in turn impacted on the case.

The purpose of such 'disclosure' is to ensure that all potential sources of evidence are made available to defendants and the courts. In criminal cases the rules are drawn from the *Police and Criminal Evidence Act 1984* and for civil cases it is drawn from the Civil Disclosure Rules and Civil Procedure Rules.

From a practical point of view the purpose of the reporting process is to ensure that reports are essentially factual and as free as possible from conjecture and opinion. Additional information may even be used out of context as part of a strategy to discredit the evidence of the victim.

RIDDOR

5.41 It is important to remember the legal requirements to report certain categories of injury under the *Reporting of Injuries, Diseases and Dangerous Occurrences Regulations 1995 (RIDDOR) (SI 1995/3163)* to the appropriate authority. These are covered in detail in CHAPTER 2.

Case study – risk assessment and reporting

5.42

Northamptonshire Police

Northamptonshire Police has developed a comprehensive, dedicated violence reporting and monitoring process. This was designed by Peter Boatman who was awarded with the Queens Police Medal for services to 'Officer Safety'. The report form is straightforward to fill in following a 'tick-box' approach for the most part, and it asks for specific information on issues such as techniques or tactics used. Factors relating to the safety of officers, bystanders, and those subject to police action/ arrest are covered.

This information is loaded into a specially designed database that can be interrogated to draw patterns and statistics as required by management. Management reports are easily generated by the database and officer safety co-ordinator.

(cont'd)

By addressing issues identified within the reporting process much has been achieved over an eight-year period. Injury rates to officers and aggressive members of the public fell to their lowest level, as did lost working days due to assaults and complaints against police. Throughout the period positive results were attained through continuously developing highly effective skills and equipment.

Notwithstanding the enhanced safety to officers and the public, the outstanding benefit accrued has been the ability of the force to evidence the need for and the reasons why skills and equipment are adopted amended or discarded. They are utilising information gained as a result of the experience of operational officers and so have the commitment of those officers in further developing the officer safety programmes, including the testing and adopting new equipment.

Checklist

5.43

Reporting

❑   Designing the system – Essential elements:

- A dedicated workplace violence incident report form.
- An investigation process.
- An information database and analysis process.
- A workplace violence co-ordinator.
- A communication process.

❑   Implementation:

- Management involved.
- Staff trained.
- Forms and report processes resourced and available.
- Reporting monitored and reviewed.

❑   Process reviewed, action taken to adjust strategy, policy, risk assessments and procedures accordingly.

❑   All documents, including reports, are subject to disclosure rules.

❑   Reporting certain incidents of violence to the relevant authorities is a legal requirement (*RIDDOR* requirements).

Key points

5.44

Assessing the risk of workplace violence

There are three basic ways in which risk of violence can be assessed:

- Generic violence risk assessment of role.
- Risk assessment of pre-planned event.
- Dynamic Risk Assessment.

Risk assessment – Who should do it?

- Front line personnel are best placed to understand risks.
- Assess in conjunction with a trained risk assessor experienced in violence management.

Risk assessment model

- Step 1 – Identify the risks inherent in the role and plan consultation.
- Step 2 – Research of incidents and identification of who may be harmed.
- Step 3 – Examine risks relating to specific activities/ tasks.
- Step 4 – Identify and examine existing risk reduction measures.
- Step 5 – Identify and implement new risk reduction measures.

Reporting system – Key elements

- A dedicated workplace violence incident report form.
- An investigation process.
- An information database and analysis process.
- A workplace violence co-ordinator.
- A communication process.

Implementation

- Manager involvement.
- Staff training.
- Provision of resources.
- Monitoring the completion of reports.

6   Risk Reduction

Introduction

6.1   Violence at work can have a devastating impact on the individuals involved and the organisation itself. Earlier chapters have outlined the importance of understanding the nature and extent of the problem and in developing a clear policy and implementation strategy.

CHAPTER 5 RISK ASSESSMENT AND REPORTING emphasised the obligations placed upon organisations to assess the risks that their staff face in relation to abuse and violence. That chapter also provided a 5-step model which outlined a number of practical ways in which risks can be identified and categorised.

This chapter will focus upon steps four and five of the model:

- Identify and examine existing risk reduction measures.

- Identify and implement new risk reduction measures.

Risk reduction is all about prevention. It may not be possible to completely eradicate violence in a workplace but it is possible to minimise the risk of violence and it's impact by introducing appropriate measures and controls. There are many ways in which risks can be reduced and some measures are specific to particular organisations and situations. Some measures are highly specialised making use of modern technology and equipment, some are a matter of 'distilled common sense' and some require an investment in the training and development of vulnerable staff. Effective risk reduction is a blend of measures which embraces all the areas of policy, effective risk assessment, practice and procedures, training, equipment, design and layout. Most sector-professional bodies offer specific guidance on the types of risk reduction measures that are appropriate within their type of organisation and useful contacts can be found in the APPENDIX. There is little point in 're-inventing the wheel' and it is a good idea to contact organisations operating in a similar sector that may have already found solutions.

There are, however, some generic measures that can be introduced and these should considered by all organisations. This chapter will cover these measures in the two areas of service delivery and security, after first examining the issue of achieving a balance when introducing appropriate measures.

Risk reduction – achieving a balance

6.2   Appropriate risk reduction measures are a balance between understanding the identified risk and providing a balanced response in terms of acceptability, cost and relative effectiveness. This is not an easy equation to balance and it requires some thought before a reduction measure is introduced. The different ways of identifying the risk have been covered comprehensively in CHAPTER 5 and this chapter will offer a range of generic risk reduction measures that can be considered across all organisations. The appropriate balance is, in the end, a matter of judgement, which can only be made by the organisation itself. The issue of glass screens is a common example of this balance eg the risk of violence has been identified – the member of staff is dealing with someone who is claiming a benefit – the claimant may not be granted it and may therefore become violent. The cost of the screen may be relatively modest and the simple balance may suggest it should be installed. However, other aspects can be added to the equation; is a glass screen acceptable in terms of the organisation's ethos and approach? Does it, in fact, reduce the level of violence – or does it provide a trigger for the level of aggression to increase? On the other hand, if there is a high risk of serious violence involving weapons at that particular location, this may outweigh other considerations and it may be imperative that a toughened glass screen is in place.

Service delivery

6.3   Workplace conflict can occur for many different reasons. Some of the causes stem directly from the personal circumstances, control, health or well being of the aggressor and are beyond the control of the organisation or staff who are confronting the individual concerned. Sometimes, however, organisations and staff can create or exacerbate the environment within which a conflict develops and increase the risk of violence by the way they deliver services or approach their work.

There is a build up to the majority of violent incidents, and often the most significant action that can be taken to reduce violence is to provide a high quality service. For example, customers, clients or patients can understandably become very frustrated over delays, cancellations or waiting times and usually it is the lack if information that fuels the frustration. When their frustration is not dealt with to their satisfaction the situation can all too easily escalate. Providing timely information may be all that is needed to placate and calm agitated service users.

This section will look at the following risk reduction measures that impact on service delivery and the value of being creative and proactive in this area.

- Training.

- Working practice.

- Systems and procedures.

- Communications (internal and external).

- Design and layout.

- Proactive service delivery.

- Problem solving.

- Warning 'flags'.

Training

6.4   The whole area of training and development is comprehensively covered in CHAPTER 7. It is mentioned here because it is a risk reduction measure in its own right by, for example, providing vulnerable staff with skills in assessing and responding to a perceived risk, improved skills for communicating in tense situations and practising physical interventions in high risk situations. Training also underpins the effective use of almost every other risk reduction measure. Good 'customer care' training, for example, will provide staff with the right attitudes and behaviours to deal with the potentially difficult customer.

Working practice

Staffing levels and work methods

6.5   Queuing and apparent 'queue jumping', long waiting times, cancellations, missed connections and flights, poorly informed staff and rude or abrupt service are all the common sparks which can eventually ignite violence. Many of these situations occur through poor service delivery and staffing levels. Wherever possible, organisations should ensure that ratios of staff to customer, client or service user are realistic and allow for the cost effective provision of the best service. This is a difficult balance to achieve in the current climate of most organisations, whether public or private, particularly where staff are probably the most expensive resource. It is easy to see the short-term attraction of reducing staffing levels but the longer term effects should not be underestimated.

Under-staffing is likely to lead to increased pressure, reduction in the quality of service provided and a consequent increased risk of dissatisfaction and conflict. Fewer staff also means less support available should a violent situation occur.

Roles should be realistically assessed for risk across all the tasks and situations that might occur. The risk assessment may show, for example, that the highest levels of risk occur on specific days and at particular times of day. An appropriate risk reduction measure might be to double up staff only across those particular times. Paired working may provide comfort to staff and be an appropriate safety measure at times, but it does not automatically reduce the risk of violence and in some cases will be neither desirable nor practicable. When staff are working side by side it is important they operate effectively as a team in conflict and risk situations, and this should be addressed in training.

Some roles have inherent risks associated with lone working, for example; visiting people in their homes and small business premises, especially when involved in some sort of enforcement or inspection role. The risks of violence may be assessed as low in terms of likelihood and frequency and therefore paired working may not be appropriate because of cost. However, there are a range of low cost and effective risk reduction measures examined in this chapter that can be introduced, and used in conjunction with safe working practices and procedures.

Safe practice guidance

6.6 Specific guidance needs to be available for each area of work to ensure its relevance. Safe practice and communication systems need to be put in place for workers based in central locations, for those working alone, and for those working out in the community who can be isolated and vulnerable to crime. Practical measures and advice should be in place to help staff reduce risk and fear when travelling to and from work, and when visiting homes. Such guidance tends to be 'common sense' but unfortunately it is not always common practice, and unless safe practice becomes a habit it will have little value.

As with any element of the strategy for managing violence, it is important to evaluate the extent to which staff follow guidance, and to ensure that managers reinforce it through example. Managers and staff need to be clear that by ignoring guidance they are not only putting themselves at risk, they are leaving themselves open to criticism and litigation. The practice, for example, of 'ringing in' to the office after the last visit before going home is useless if it is only followed intermittently.

There is a plethora of guidance in the form of safe practice tips in every sector, and whilst this will provide a useful reference, staff are more likely to adopt guidance that they have actually been involved in developing. This guidance will be workable and directly relevant, and staff will be more committed to it. Some general tips are included at the end of this chapter.

Systems and procedures

6.7   Violent crime and violence towards workers is on the increase. For instance, minor problems with customers can all too easily escalate especially when alcohol is involved. Those working in certain urban areas may be more likely to be exposed to theft, robbery, aggressive begging, prostitution, public disorder, drug dealing and drug abuse. Rural areas present different challenges, as staff can be a long way from help, for example, when confronted by angry landowners.

Some roles, particularly in health care, necessarily involve close contact with a person to carry out checks, tests and medical procedures. Some workers, rail operators and airlines for example, deal with aggressive people in confined spaces where there are risks to other people and little prospect of immediate help from the police or security staff.

Effective risk assessment will anticipate and deal proactively with situations likely to cause conflict. High demands on service, running out of stock, maintenance work likely to cause delays, and particularly unpalatable news, are some of the situations that can be anticipated and contingencies for minimising and resolving conflict put in place.

A thorough risk assessment of all aspects of a particular role will unearth the situations and activities that present special risks such as:

- Delivering unwelcome or 'bad news' in various forms.

- Cash handling.

- Refusing entry or evicting trespassers.

- Contact with criminals.

- Certain aspects of lone and community-based work.

- Contact with individuals whose behaviour is unpredictable due to a psychiatric or medical condition or treatment.

- Dealing with persons influenced by alcohol or drugs.

- Necessary 'close contact' with unpredictable people.

- Dealing with aggressive or unpredictable individuals in confined spaces or where help is not easily available.

Each risk should be examined and appropriate guidance and practice designed which will minimise the risks involved in the working practice or situation. Guidance and procedures need to be put in place for staff performing such activities, and appropriate training given on how to reduce risk and manage conflict and violence.

Case study

Retail and licensed: Risk reduction systems and procedures

An example of the guidance and procedures that can be introduced as risk reduction measures can be found in the retail and licensed sectors. Both sectors are experiencing increasing violence in shops, supermarkets, restaurants, hotels, bars and nightclubs. Some of the measures they are taking include:

- Varying banking times and methods ie disguising the process.

- Keeping strict security when 'cashing up' and ensuring front and back doors are locked.

- Identifying and reducing common causes of conflict with customers.

- Developing safe practice procedures for vulnerable situations, such as 'drinking up' time, dealing with thieves and trouble-makers, opening and closing the venue.

- Developing communication links with other local businesses and the police.

- Discouraging problem elements such as those:

    o   Seeking an 'office' for illegitimate activities such as drug dealing, prostitution, or handling stolen goods.

    o   Aggressive begging.

    o   Using drugs in open areas and toilets.

Continuous learning

6.8   Staff at all levels need to be encouraged to debrief regularly and to look for improvements to working practices and procedures. Line managers need to possess basic operational debriefing skills, and feedback mechanisms need to be put in place to ensure best practice is gathered and shared. Specific responsibilities need to be given ensuring that learning and continuous improvement becomes a habit, and that inadequacies are exposed.

This continuous learning will only be possible in an open 'no blame' culture, where staff do not fear being criticised when they report problems. Positive feedback is also vital to encourage staff to present concerns and offer ideas on possible solutions.

CHAPTER 9 examines post-incident issues and reinforces the importance of being sensitive not to blame the victim when reviewing violent incidents, and to focus instead on supporting the individual and to find ways of preventing a reoccurrence.

Some airlines are working hard to create 'no blame' cultures and actively encourage the reporting of 'near misses' so that learning can be drawn from them. British Airways encouraged staff to report incidents including disruptive behaviour, by paying overtime when staff could not complete reports on their tour of duty. It is also important to ensure that staff do not suffer financial penalty through missed work as a result of supporting a prosecution.

Communications (external and internal)

6.9   Poor information and communications both internally and externally, often causes or contributes to conflict. Effective communication can quickly calm and resolve potential conflict. Many people will accept the inevitability of a delay or cancellation – as long as they know how long it will be or what alternatives are available. The most dangerous situations often stem from the frustrated customer who cannot get information, action or satisfaction from 'the organisation' and turns his or her anger directly and personally upon the member of staff trying to deal with the situation.

External communications can target:

- Service users.
- Non-service users whom staff may come into contact with.
- Other agencies such as the police and local authority.
- Media sources.
- Other local employers.

A number of these aspects have been covered already in CHAPTER **4**, and range from providing up to date information on the service and any delays or difficulties to users, to communication of the consequences of acts of violence towards staff. Posters are commonly used to warn of the consequences of assaulting employees and this should be in simple unambiguous terms, as demonstrated by the current London Underground poster (see figure 6.1 below).

To avoid conflict it is important that organisations constantly manage the expectations of service users. These expectations may at times be unrealistic and fuelled by the media or unachievable customer or patient 'charters', but staff can influence the outcome of the situation by the way they respond at an interpersonal level.

Effective internal communications between management and staff and between departments will reduce mistakes and misunderstandings that

Figure 6.1: London Underground poster warning of prosecution

impact on the service user and in turn on conflict and risk. The importance of sharing information on known violent individuals is explored later in this chapter. Internal conflicts between staff are a cause of communication breakdown and considerable misery all around. These conflicts often exist below the surface of relationships between individual staff and between departments. Managers and staff usually know where internal conflicts exist but are generally reluctant to address these difficult issues that are so close to home, it is far easier to confront external issues. As with bullying, internal conflict requires different management strategies that are not covered in this handbook. Advice on this area is available on the following website: www.workplaceviolence.co.uk.

Design and layout

6.10   Design and layout impact directly on service delivery, and can, with a little thought, reduce the likelihood of problems occurring and make it easier to manage those that do. Designers are becoming more aware of the issue of work-related violence and significant developments are being made in this area as it becomes clear that personal safety and good service delivery go hand in hand. Some pub chains for example use clever layouts to reduce potential frustrations and conflict flash points, thereby 'enhancing the customer experience', selling more drinks and reducing the risk of violence and aggression.

The layout and ambience will influence both the attitudes of staff and the customer or service user. Interestingly, greater respect seems to be shown for property in a smart, well cared for environment, and many service points experience less hostility when they remove their screens and develop an open plan layout. There are workplaces where screens are essential controls, so it is important that decisions are not taken rashly.

Colour choice, furnishings, lighting and background music all have an impact and improvements can be made, even on limited budgets. Waiting areas can be made more comfortable and utilise information screens, pay phones, televisions (controlled by staff), drink/ snack dispensers, magazines and children's entertainment. 'Queue jumping' is a very common cause of conflict and effective signage and queue management can reduce this.

Many organisations have met with staff resistance when removing security screens and going open plan. Staff can fear that they will have nothing to protect them from the people who once attacked the screens. Following the removal of the screens and the provision of appropriate training, staff are usually pleasantly surprised; the barriers to communication have been removed, service improves and so do the customers! A carefully planned consultative process needs to be adopted to ensure a smooth transition. Recently industrial action was experienced at a major countrywide agency over plans to remove protective screens.

The situation could well have been prevented if staff had been properly consulted and management had addressed their fears sensitively and effectively.

Risk can be further reduced with the introduction of wider desks, raised floors, and areas offering access to those with special needs or requiring greater privacy. Clever lattice work can secure staff areas, and both theft and criminal damage reduced through fixed furnishings and desktop equipment. Staff need to have access to a secure place should a serious incident occur, and private areas need to be clearly identified and secured.

To help to deter drug abuse in toilets and others areas, specific fluorescent tubes can be fitted that make it difficult for those injecting to locate veins, and the smooth surfaces needed by cocaine users can be reduced.

Employees are often concerned about the security of their vehicles and their personal safety when walking through car parks. The design of car parks, and the effective use of access control, CCTV and lighting are well researched. Well designed car parks can earn the Association of Chief Police Officers (ACPO) Secured Car Park Award. The British Parking Association administers the scheme and can provide guidance on it.

Proactive service delivery

6.11   The quality of service delivery has a major bearing on the incidence of violence in the workplace. A climate for trouble is created when people are frustrated; their expectations are not met and staff respond unprofessionally to their concerns. Some people need little justification for their aggressive and violent behaviour.

Sometimes, staff cannot meet the customers' expectations because of circumstances beyond their control. The response should be to influence and adjust the customer expectation. The right skills can turn a dissatisfied customer/ service user into loyal friend, simply by staff responding to their concerns.

The development of these basic interpersonal skills and a service oriented culture lays the foundations for a safer environment. This area is probably the most under-rated as a control measure.

A lack of up to date information for travellers or people in waiting areas is a common cause of frustration. If people know how long they have to wait, they can consider their options and make an informed decision. Staff can become defensive or retreat into their shells when delays occur, as most understandably dislike conflict. This unfortunately creates an air of distrust between staff and service users. It is invariably in everyone's interest to take a proactive stance and:

- Get out and talk to service users.

- Listen and empathise with their concerns.

- Be open and honest – 'tell it as it is'.

- Apologise and accept responsibility when appropriate.

- If possible, offer alternatives or concessions.

Simple inexpensive gestures like providing refreshments, upgrades, free use of a telephone or concessions can help to reduce tension, and it is important that staff are empowered to offer these (with appropriate support guidance).

Problem solving

6.12   To be effective in reducing risk it is important to understand the root causes of the problem and not merely the symptoms. This will prevent waste in terms of time and resources on ineffective solutions. When responding to concerns over violence, organisations often 'throw' money at one element of strategy such as training or security, which has limited impact on the problem. The simplest way to get to the root cause of many problems is to ask the 'Five Whys', for example:

1.   Why did the person become abusive?

    'Because she was angry and completely lost it'.

2.   Why was she angry?

    'She was kept waiting and then she couldn't get what she wanted'.

3.   Why was she kept waiting?

    'We were short staffed'.

4.   Why were we short staffed?

    'Because the management never plan for school half term'.

5.   Why didn't we have what she wanted?

    'We didn't anticipate the demand or check our supply'.

In one real life example an organisation was looking to increase security following an assault – in other words deal with the symptoms. Five 'why' questions exposed the real problem, identified a real solution, and saved a lot of money.

Many organisations experience problems with a particular individual or group of patients or service users. It is important to be able to anticipate problems and to respond quickly to the risks presented. Organisations providing residential care will often have care plans for each individual client, and staff will know triggers to avoid and positive behaviours that the client responds to.

Other workers often know little or nothing about the people they come into contact with and rely on safe practice and their dynamic risk assessment. Where potential risks become apparent there should be a simple mechanism in place that triggers an immediate review and puts in place control measures. This will prevent a situation where a violent individual could be involved in a number of violent incidents at a hostel, care home or hospital, before controls are put in place.

Although security plays an important part in staff safety, sometimes creative and inexpensive solutions can often be found to problems. A building society branch in London that had been a victim of a spate of armed robberies demonstrated this. The manager contacted local police stations and let it be known that coffee and doughnuts would be available to officers passing by in acknowledgement of their support during this difficult period. The regular appearance of police cars outside the building society probably played a role in deterring would be criminals – and the robberies stopped.

Cause – effect thinking

6.13   So often decisions are taken in organisations without considering the possible impact at the point of service delivery. A classic example, is the 'smoking ban'. In today's climate, particularly in the UK, smoking is generally considered to be an anti-social activity. The entrance areas of many business premises bear testimony to this with hardy souls braving wind, rain and cold for their nicotine top up. Most organisations now limit smoking to certain areas, and some go further – some hospital trusts have banned smoking on an entire hospital site. Such decisions are clearly based on sound principles – a healthcare environment cannot condone an activity that has such an adverse effect on health. However, a 'blanket policy' such as this actually has a substantial impact in terms of risk reduction for aggression and violence. For example, staff working on a short-stay admissions ward may be dealing with a patient who is suffering the effects of withdrawal from drugs or alcohol abuse. The patient is already agitated and frustrated and desperate for a cigarette. No dedicated smoking area is available and the individual is becoming increasingly aggressive. Stretched nursing staff can only reduce the risk by escorting the patient out of the hospital.

Staff in hospitals and other organisations are regularly subjected to verbal abuse, threats, and physical assault when enforcing smoking rules and managers need to recognise this when forming policy. This is not a plea for the pro-smoking lobby – it is a plea for recognition of the practical implications of introducing well meaning measures and providing for the possible consequences of enforcing such a policy.

Warning 'flags'

6.14 A contentious issue for many organisations is the placing of warning 'flags' against an individual service user or address. Many organisations cite client/ patient confidentiality, data protection and human rights as reasons for not placing warnings. Some also argue that if staff know someone could be a problem then this will affect the way they deal with them and risk a self fulfilling prophecy. Although each of these issues is valid and needs to be considered, employees also have rights and a balance must be sought in order to ensure staff safety.

Data protection agencies provide guidance on the use of such warning systems and their management.

Airlines are pressing for a central system that shares information on disruptive passengers, to prevent a situation whereby a violent passenger barred from one airline, can book a seat with another unaware carrier.

Large and diverse organisations such as local authorities are linking computer systems or providing a central collation of information to enable workers in different areas to make safety checks before meeting a service user. The need for such a system is highlighted by the instance where a housing officer was assaulted visiting a service user who was known to be violent by social services staff in the same authority. This type of situation is avoidable and employers could find themselves in court by failing to address it.

Key points

6.15

Risk reduction through service delivery

- Training – is a key risk reduction measure for:
    - ○ establishing good practice and procedures;
    - ○ soft skills development and good customer service;
    - ○ physical intervention skills; and
    - ○ use of equipment.
- Working practice – matters to consider are work methods, appropriate staffing levels and guidance on safe practice.
- Systems and procedures – can be created to meet identifiable and foreseen risks.

(cont'd)

- Communications – necessary for:

    o   educating the service user of sanctions etc if violence is used towards staff.

    o   Internal communication about unsafe practice etc.

- Design and layout – 'designing in' safer environments including better layout, information, CCTV etc.

- Proactive service delivery – taking the initiative by meeting the problems early and head on eg providing customers with information if there are delays.

- Problem solving – identify the real cause of the problem not just the symptoms.

- Warning 'flags' – don't write off as 'too much trouble'. There are safeguards about confidentiality and data protection but they do not prevent the use of warning flags.

Security responses

6.16 Physical security measures and security staff provide another key element of a strategic response to violence. Effective security will help to deter those persons considering crime or violence and subsequently reduce risks to staff and service users. There are initiatives in place to raise standards within the security industry, the reputation of which has suffered at the hands of some less than professional providers. The Private Security Industry Bill is having a fundamental impact on the industry, and providers will have to satisfy certain criteria if they are to be licensed to operate. The new Security Industry Authority is actively establishing standards that will include the minimum level of training for security staff performing specific roles such as door supervision or parking enforcement.

Some organisations have their own security manager, whilst others rely on external consultants for advice on different aspects of security. This section will look at the security responses available to organisations in three areas:

- Security personnel.

- Procedures.

- Physical measures.

Security personnel

6.17 The scope of the security industry is expanding rapidly as roles that were traditionally the domain of police and prison services are being privatised, such as:

- Parking enforcement.

- Community and street wardens.

- Response to intruder alarms.

- Management of prisons, courts and remand centres.

Police and prison officers who traditionally performed these functions underwent very comprehensive selection and training and it is important that those now adopting these roles are also properly selected and trained. In some ways, the work can be more challenging for non-police staff because the people they deal with know that they do not have the same authority and ultimate sanction of the police.

Some organisations use external security contractors, others choose to employ an in-house team or mix the two. There are benefits and drawbacks to each.

If considering an external provider it is important to establish the level of investment that the provider makes in staff training and support. In a traditionally low paid area of work with a high turnover of staff, contractors are reluctant to invest in more than the bare minimum required for training. Any tender offer and subsequent contract should clearly define the expectations of the role and stipulate the requirements relating to training and service delivery. As with the outsourcing of training, it is important to seek best value rather than base a decision on cost alone.

More control over selection, training and performance is achieved through developing an in-house security team. Whichever option is chosen it is important to remember that security staff can't work effectively in isolation. They need to be actively involved in the initiatives, so that they can win the trust and support of other staff and made to feel part of the team.

It is very easy for managers and staff to abdicate their personal responsibilities where dedicated security staff exist, and to say 'that's a security problem'. In reality however the most effective security will only be possible where all staff recognise that they also have a responsibility to be vigilant and to embrace security measures. Security staff need to be part of a wider staff team and involved in the continuous development of good practice. There are also benefits to including security staff in training events concerned with preventing and managing violence.

Selection

6.18 Security staff, by the very nature of their role, will deal with conflict on a regular basis. Their attitudes and behaviour are vital to their ability to deal lawfully, appropriately and successfully with conflict situations. Developing the 'right attitude' in an individual through a training programme is a difficult, if not impossible, task – particularly in the short term. It is important therefore to select staff who demonstrate the attitudes and behaviours that help to deal positively with situations where conflict is inevitable.

Some organisations have quite sophisticated recruitment and selection systems, which target behaviours as part of the overall selection process. Many, however, rely on an application form, 'paper sift' and a formal interview with a final selection of candidates to select staff.

The ideal way of selecting staff is to put candidates through a series of work-related situations, which will test their ability, skills and attitudes when dealing with typical situations. If this is not possible in-house, there are a number of consultants who can provide expertise and staff to develop and run an assessment centre for selecting staff. As always, it is important to be sure that consultants are experienced in the relevant area and that expectations can be met. Testimony from other organisations that they have worked with is probably the most effective means of establishing this.

Training

6.19   Formal training within the security industry tends to be NVQ based. 'Soft skills' such as conflict management, interpersonal, defusing and assertiveness skills cannot be easily measured. This critical interpersonal aspect of the work is often neglected. Security staff play a key role in service delivery and are often the first and last point of contact for a customer or service user. It is therefore a worthwhile investment to develop their communication skills.

The British Institute of Innkeeping has demonstrated through the National Certificate For Door Supervisors – Licensed Premises, that these vital soft skills can form a key part of qualifications when taught in a dynamic way.

CHAPTER 7 looks in detail at how training needs can be assessed and effective training designed and delivered. It is important to emphasise here the need to equip security staff and other employees that adopt a security role, with the necessary knowledge and skills to manage conflict and violent behaviour. Security staff are often expected to confront potential criminals, respond to violent situations, and to protect staff and service users. It is ironic that they often receive less training than the staff they are expected to support when problems occur.

By the very nature of the security role, those performing it will need to be properly equipped, and trained in how to reduce risk and manage violent situations. This training will at the very least include personal safety awareness and conflict management training, and an understanding of key aspects of the law concerning the use of force. Where there is likelihood that they will be expected to remove trespassers, apprehend thieves or control physically violent individuals, they must be trained further in the appropriate physical interventions relating to these tasks, and their safe and lawful use. Failure to provide appropriate training in these areas could result in prosecution or substantial litigation by the security officer or another person affected by their action or inaction.

It is not unusual for employees to perform security functions as part of their role, an example is that of hospital porters. Whether this role is defined in job specifications (which it should be) or has simply been 'assumed' – it is essential that the staff member is adequately trained to perform it.

Case study

Hastings Borough Council: Staff selection and training

Hastings Borough Council intended to recruit a team of eight street wardens and one senior street warden. The importance of selecting the right people from the start was recognised and they sought help from external consultants to assist with the recruiting process. The consultants took the job descriptions and created a skills matrix for the roles. They then developed a three-stage assessment centre. In the first stage, each candidate had to deal with a role-play incident involving a typical conflict situation that might be experienced by a street warden. The second stage involved writing a report about the incident, and the third stage involved a discussion group with other candidates about topics associated with the role. Assessors scored and provided written feedback about the performance of each candidate against the skills matrix. Each candidate went on to have an interview with internal staff and the information from the assessment centre was made available to the interviewers and used as part of the final selection. The assessment centre accommodated 16 candidates and ran from 9.00 am to 4 pm.

The external consultant also assisted in the subsequent training programme for the successful candidates.

Key learning achieved through the assessment centre:

- The assessment centre tested soft skills such as the individual's behaviour and approach to managing conflict, non-verbal and verbal communication skills, assertiveness and report writing skills.

(cont'd)

- The information gained at the assessment centre helped the interviewers to explore areas of concern about behaviours and attitudes evidenced during the stages.

- The data from the assessment centre was scored and evidenced in a way that could be used in the final selection of the candidates.

- The marks and written feedback provided the basis of an individual training needs' analysis for the subsequent development of each successful candidate.

- The marks and written feedback could provide unsuccessful candidates with areas to improve for subsequent applications.

- Assessment centres can be achieved in reasonable times scales and at reasonable cost.

Procedures

6.20 Security staff face very difficult and sometimes dangerous situations where their actions may be subjected to detailed scrutiny. It is important therefore that staff are clear as to the expectations upon them for preventing and responding to violent incidents. Clear procedures need to be put in place for each role that outline the action to be taken in areas such as:

- Risk reduction.

- Incident management.

- Post-incident management.

- Refusing entry and evicting persons.

- Making an arrest.

- Searching people and premises.

- Responding to alarms.

- Confiscation of drugs.

- Protecting evidence.

- Cash handling.

- CCTV management.

- Reporting.

The procedure is only the beginning. There is also a need to ensure that every member of staff who performs such a role is aware of and understands each procedure. This might be done through a variety of ways including formal training, coaching, internal communication systems, posters, personal issue of memo cards and management briefing.

Other employees will also need guidance as to what they can expect of their security colleagues, and how they can help security staff when the need arises. This will help to prevent a breakdown in communication when an incident takes place, and uncertainty over issues such as who should take control of the situation.

CHAPTER 8 INCIDENT MANAGEMENT highlights the importance of re-hearsing and testing the response to incidents, and this provides another excellent opportunity to develop teamwork and to clarify roles and expectations.

Venue/site managers should take an active interest in contract security staff to ensure:

- Consistent application of procedures and 'house rules'.

- High standards of customer service.

- Effective cross-team communications.

- Reporting and accountability.

- Contract security staff are supported.

Where arrests are likely, such as in retail environments, it is important that security staff have access to an appropriate location where the subject can be detained until the police arrive. Consideration needs to be given to the layout of the area that should be clear of potential weapons and have a means of summoning help in an emergency.

Physical measures

6.21   There is a vast range of physical measures that can be introduced to reduce the risk of physical injury through a workplace violence incident and many of these are outlined in the next sections.

Some of these measures can be extremely expensive and it is worth emphasising here that a thorough risk assessment needs to be undertaken before committing to any expenditure on specialised equipment. There are plenty of suppliers waiting to provide the most up to date piece of kit and it as important to know what the risks are so that an evaluation can be made about the appropriateness and effectiveness of the equipment being offered. Analysis of information about incidents, for example the type of injures sustained and parts of the body affected, will provide vital information for the decision-making process.

Physical security and safety equipment

Access control

6.22   Although most organisations do not wish to turn buildings into fortresses, there is a need for some form of access control to protect people and property. There are many variations possible ranging from barriers to open plan receptions; however funding and existing building design are major influences on this. A well-designed and managed reception can contribute greatly to access control, yet be seen as offering a friendly and helpful service rather than looking intimidating and overtly tight on security.

A key part of access control is the ability to distinguish intruders from legitimate users within the building. Identity systems can help, but need to be well designed, and simple to operate and enforce.

Case study

Train operating companies

The benefits of access control are being seen on the railway where research has shown that the majority of people involved in crime and nuisance on the railway do not have tickets. Staff face high levels of violence in some areas and those working on trains and in revenue protection roles are most vulnerable to abuse and physical assault.

A number of rail companies have invested heavily in the installation of automatic ticket gates (similar to those seen on the London Underground) in order to reduce fare evasion and the crime and violence associated with it. These gates are proving effective when they form part of a wider, integrated range of risk reduction measures including:

- Closed circuit television (CCTV).

- Risk assessment of 'hotspots' such as ticket barriers.

- Panic alarms and mobile phones.

- Revenue protection initiatives.

- Clear messages about the consequences of violence towards staff.

- Staff training in personal safety and conflict management.

- Improved customer information and service delivery.

- Partnership with British Transport Police.

Closed circuit television (CCTV)

6.23   Although the outlay on CCTV can be high, it is one of the most popular security responses available for deterring and managing crime and violence. Depending on the intended purpose, relatively inexpensive portable systems can also be used in certain areas. A recent Home Office commissioned report suggests that CCTV is more effective as a detection tool than as a deterrent. Organisations therefore need to be realistic about its purpose and use. For effective prevention it therefore desirable that CCTV is monitored and used proactively. Glasgow city centre and London's Oxford Street have seen the use of CCTV in such a proactive manner, and the London Borough of Newham is another leading exponent of CCTV technology.

The effectiveness of CCTV depends greatly on the type of system and its suitability for the intended purpose. The right equipment in competent hands will allow key areas to be monitored, incidents controlled, intelligence gathered and evidence recorded. It is important that guidelines exist on the use of CCTV and the management of recordings, to ensure that valuable evidence is not compromised.

Take care to establish what the organisation wants the system to do and remember that poor lighting, or the wrong match of lens, monitor and/ or recorder will compromise its effectiveness.

When selecting a system bear in mind that some providers may be more interested in selling boxes of equipment than providing a solution to the problem. Seek advice from security managers in other organisations and be sure of the organisation's requirements.

Alarms

6.24   There are many types of alarm system, each designed for a different purpose. Before purchasing, be sure of the organisation's needs and consider them in the strategy for tackling violence. Although alarms may act as a deterrent in the eyes of a potential offender, they tend to be reactive – indicating that something has occurred.

The key alarm systems involved with enhancing personal safety are:

- Intruder alarms – commonly used to protect buildings after hours, or to protect restricted areas. These help to prevent or give warning of unlawful entry, and thereby reduce the likelihood of staff members being confronted by potentially dangerous individuals.

- Panic alarms – increasingly used in reception areas, interview rooms and isolated areas (often covertly). Be sure to locate them intelligently and have procedures in place so that staff know how to respond to an alarm.

- Personal alarms – carried on the person as a means of attracting attention and temporarily distracting an assailant. The products vary from the low budget audible item to the optimal system-linked portable panic alarm. The effectiveness of the basic audible alarm will vary with each situation; they are only of use if at hand and should never be viewed as a quick remedy or substitute for preventive measures. Unfortunately, once initial interest has subsided many staff either do not bother to carry their alarms or keep them to hand.

Radios, paging and public address systems

6.25   These communication systems have advanced greatly in recent years and can be an asset to staff safety. Some personal radios and pagers have built in panic alarms and sophisticated tracking facilities that pinpoint the location of the unit. The system needs to be carefully selected and staff trained in its use; radio systems can get people into trouble as well as out of it; radio discipline is vital and appropriate language and codes need to be adopted. Manufacturers may provide basic advice and training but this is unlikely to be comprehensive.

Mobile phones

6.26   Mobile phones can provide a means of communication and comfort to lone workers. They are useful for keeping colleagues informed of movements and of unforeseen travel/ schedule difficulties. However, as with alarms, they are not a solution, and can be difficult to use in a violent situation. It is important to programme key numbers into the memory for recall in difficult situations.

Protective vests

6.27   Often referred to as 'body armour' these vests can be designed to protect against the threats presented by firearms (ballistic threats) and edged weapons (such as knives and other sharp items that can be used to stab or slash). Protective vests can also provide trauma protection (from blows and kicks), and are designed to be worn either covertly (under clothing) or overtly – as commonly seen on police officers.

Other organisations can purchase protective vests as no specific authority or licence is required, and they can be a necessary risk reduction measure in some areas of work. It is however important that the decision to adopt protective vests is not taken lightly, as it can be a sensitive issue for employees, purchasers of services, and the public generally. Great care needs to be taken when considering purchasing this expensive equipment and effective risk assessment, incident reporting and monitoring processes will indicate:

- Whether it is needed – or is it a knee jerk response to violent incidents?

- When it is needed – should everybody wear it all the time?

- The level of protection it should offer – is the threat from firearms, edged weapons, strikes and kicks, or a combination of these?

- Should it be worn overtly or covertly – is it important that the vest is not seen?

The vest needs to fit the wearer properly if it is to provide proper protection, and it should be borne in mind that if it is uncomfortable it is less likely to be worn. It is ironic that some organisations have bought vests that offer high protection against most threats, yet staff have found these bulky vests uncomfortable and rarely wear them. Some protection is clearly better than none, and advances in materials and design allows for an effective balance of protection and comfort.

The vest size, design, weight, and practicality are key considerations, for example does it allow the range of movement needed by the wearer in their job? Vests also need to be designed specifically for female wearers. Vests that offer protection against both firearms and edged weapons are usually more substantial than those protecting against firearms alone.

The best designs will include pockets for equipment such as radios and job specific tools such as those needed by ambulance staff or police officers. Some organisations issue vests for specific operations or provide shared access to them for use when an incident occurs. The problem with this approach is that staff may have to wear a vest that does not fit properly, and there is also a hygiene issue associated with sharing. Another problem is that some incidents can occur with little warning and staff may not have the opportunity to put on the vest.

The most desirable option is personal issue as this overcomes concerns over fit and hygiene. This will of course require a substantial budget and the benefits need to be weighed alongside other risk reduction options.

A key issue is to decide when vests will be worn. Some agencies advocate that they should be worn the whole time as the threats cannot always be predicted, others specify that they should be worn at certain times or when undertaking certain tasks. The risk assessment will form the basis of such a decision.

Restraints

6.28 As the breadth of work undertaken by the security industry develops, more use is being made of restraints such as handcuffs. These are common in policing, custodial services, airlines and some areas of healthcare. Although the concept of using restraints will understandably concern most employers, they may be a necessary measure to prevent a disruptive passenger putting an aircraft at risk, or to prevent a patient harming themselves or others. Use of such equipment needs to be justified by the role requirements and risk assessments, and staff need comprehensive training and guidance in its use. It should also be subject to a detailed medical review.

Advice should be sought before adopting handcuffs and other restraints to ensure an appropriate and lawful choice is made. New restraints such as the emergency response belt are becoming popular within some areas of work, as they allow a great deal of control without pain.

A restrained person should always be kept under observation for medical reasons and also to ensure they do not escape from the restraint – nothing is infallible!

Batons

6.29   Batons are deemed offensive weapons and can only be used by the police. It is also important to realise that any object, no matter how innocent, can become an offensive weapon if the person possessing it has the intention to use it in such a way. Security staff have been known to carry large heavy metal torches 'for their own protection', and in this context these become an offensive weapon.

Case study

6.30

Northamptonshire Police

Selection and introduction of new safety equipment

CHAPTER 5 looked at the work of Inspector Boatman QPM and his team in the creation of a detailed incident reporting and monitoring system that helps the force to make accurate risk assessments and informed management decisions on personal safety issues. The value of this approach can be seen in the organisation's approach to finding the right protective equipment for its officers.

Protective vests

Northamptonshire police undertook comprehensive research and field trials before selecting the protective vest its officers would be supplied with. Six manufacturers were involved in the tender process and four,

---

three-month wearer trials were undertaken involving 20 officers (one of which was for female officers). This process helped to shape the ultimate design specification and to ensure that the vest would be practical and 'wearable'. The organisation's impressive incident reporting and monitoring process was able to inform the degree of protection required and when the vests were most needed. The primary protection needed was against edged weapons and trauma, with a lesser ballistic requirement.

The design of the end product produced by Mehler Vario Systems was greatly influenced by the wearer trials and incorporated a carriage system for equipment such as handcuffs and radios. This meant that additional utility belts were no longer needed and back problems that had been associated with these were subsequently reduced. The vest used flame retardent materials and incorporated a degree of buoyancy should an officer enter water (which has since happened).

Northamptonshire Police decided to issue every officer with a made to measure vest to ensure optimum comfort and protection. Initial evaluations showed a remarkable 100% wearer rate (other forces had experienced a rate as low as 30%). The risk assessments identified that the vests needed to be worn between 4 pm and 4 am, but most were worn all day. Trauma to the torso from strikes and kicks had previously resulted in significant officer sickness, and this was reduced to zero following the introduction of the vests.

Introduction of a new restraint device

Following a Northamptonshire Police study on post arrest injury to both officers and subjects detained, it became clear that in 14% of cases, force was used was on people who were already in handcuffs. The statistics were supported by research in two other British police forces, and highlighted how a violent person can remain a threat even when in handcuffs. To reduce this injury risk the force sought an additional restraint device that could offer greater control of an arrested person.

Peter Boatman and his team identified a device called the emergency response belt (ERB) that had been used successfully to reduce injury in American prisons, police forces and medical facilities. Northamptonshire Police decided to test the ERB and set up a three-month field trial with a 'control group'. During the trial no post-arrest injuries occurred to police or subjects, whereas in the control areas four officers and three subjects were injured and £5,000 worth of damage caused to vehicles. The use of the ERB is subject to annual review by medical consultants, and staff receive comprehensive guidance and training in its use.

(cont'd)

In the two years since the adoption of the ERB, Northamptonshire Police has:

- Reduced injuries to both officers and subjects to the lowest levels recorded.

- Received the lowest levels of complaints.

The ERB is now being widely adopted in police, security, healthcare and other agencies.

Conclusions

Northamptonshire Police has demonstrated how effective this equipment can be in some high risk areas of work. Most organisations are unlikely to need this type of equipment, but all will be able to see the value in the rigorous research and testing that Northamptonshire Police has taken before spending large sums on risk reduction measures. This organisation is able to make informed decisions and assess the effectiveness of its measures because it has high quality management information from its unique reporting and risk assessment process.

Summary

Key points

6.31

Security responses

- Security personnel

  Effective selection and training is vital to the employment of security personnel whether internally or externally provided. This matter is often neglected in the security industry – although measures are being introduced to improve standards.

- Procedures

  Security staff and those who work with them, need very clear unambiguous guidance about what to do, and what not to do, across the range of incidents and issues they may be involved in.

- Physical measures

  There are a wide range of physical measures available. Careful risk assessment, incident monitoring and analysis of information will provide the most appropriate and cost effective measures.

General safety tips

6.32

These tips are included as a general guide as to areas to consider when writing safe practice guidance. This is not intended as a definitive list, and it is important that a thorough generic and planned risk assessment (see CHAPTER 5) is carried out as the starting point for guidance. It is also important for each workplace to involve staff in developing this guidance so that it responds directly to their working situation. This process will make the advice more meaningful and it will be more likely that staff will adopt it.

At the office

- Consider the layout of the building and how someone could make a quick exit if they needed to.

- Staff should be positioned in a way to ensure best vision of the door.

- Consider security at the office and especially arrangements when working outside normal hours – remember security is everyone's responsibility.

- Identify places of safety around the building and nearby.

- Ensure that there is access to an outside line telephone.

- Plan travel to and from work carefully and link up with colleagues.

- If safe and appropriate, challenge anyone not recognised politely eg 'Can I help you?'.

- Be polite and helpful on the telephone – since anyone within the organisation could come face to face with this person later.

- If an abusive call needs to be ended, do so in a controlled and assertive manner.

- Communicate any concerns over procedures or working practice to the employer, and offer solutions.

- Report all violent incidents and harassment of any form, whether from customers or colleagues.

Meetings

6.33

Meetings at the office

Planned meetings

- Inform colleagues of a meeting and consider asking one to be present.

- Tell reception and security staff where appropriate.

- Prepare the meeting room and clear objects/ potential weapons.

- Ensure there is easy access to exits and panic alarms.

- Think through exit strategies and ways to terminate the meeting.

- Put visitors at ease and make them feel welcome.

- Be prepared for the meeting and have the necessary information/ paperwork needed to avoid upset.

- Inform the manager of any problems so that they can prepare for repercussions.

Unplanned meetings

- Ask reception/ colleagues to establish the reason for the visit, the number of visitors and their mood.

- Assess the situation and meet the visitors in an area where colleagues can see.

- If a decision is taken to go ahead with the meeting ask for a couple of minutes to find a room and follow meetings guidance.

- If unable or unwilling to hold the meeting consider the best way to explain this and offer alternative suggestions.

- Always listen, empathise and take the visitor and their situation seriously.

Working outside

6.34

Working outside the office

Before leaving

- Arrange with a colleague a system of times by which they will receive a report of movements, and give them a summary of the visits made.

- Find out as much as possible about the person with whom the meeting is with.

- Ensure that all parties are clear as to the purpose of the meeting.

- Hold meetings in public areas that feel comfortable.

- When visiting unfamiliar territory, verify details first.

- If in any doubt as to the location or the person, seek support or rearrange the meeting.

- Organise effectively to avoid difficult situations.

- Consider calling the person before the meeting to confirm arrangements and establish their mood/state.

- Consider whether a colleague should be present.

- If there is a fear for safety and controlling the risks – do not go – explain the concerns to a manager.

Personal checklist

- Carry credentials or ID, ready to show at the door straight away.

- Ensure possession of all necessary documentation required for the visit.

- Carry a personal alarm and mobile phone if possible and programme in key numbers.

- Always carry emergency cash and a phone card.

- Carry a torch if likely to be out in the dark.

- Avoid carrying things that attract criminals and do not provide them with the opportunity to commit the crime.

On the approach

- Select a parking spot carefully and position for a quick exit.

- Assess the environment before committing to it.

(cont'd

- Wait outside and listen before knocking on the door.

- Be purposeful and confident as this can deter illegitimate interest.

- Have an exit excuse prepared in case the situation feels uncomfortable.

- Show respect for other people, their property, and cultural differences.

On return

- Ensure information concerning risk is passed to other colleagues/ added to file.

- Report any incident that may have occurred.

- Review safe practice with colleagues at team meetings.

Travel safety

- Consider personal safety when making travel arrangements.

- Plan routes carefully and if there are regular schedules these should be varied.

- Select hotels/ accommodation carefully.

- Always consider various options and have a 'plan b'.

- Carry a personal alarm and a mobile phone with key numbers programmed in.

- Keep valuables out of sight.

- Appear confident and purposeful to deter potential illegitimate interest.

- If driving, ensure that the vehicle is serviced and has sufficient fuel.

- In the event of a vehicle breaking down use a mobile phone; on a motorway stand on the embankment but lock yourself in the car if someone approaches (and talk through a small gap in window).

- On buses and trains select a seat carefully near others. Be prepared to move.

- Possess taxi numbers, and ascertain the details of the driver being sent.

- Carry enough cash for a journey and some extra for emergencies.

7   Training

Introduction

7.1   Providing effective training is an essential element of an employer's duty of care to employees. Through training employees can identify ways in which they can reduce risk and develop the skills they need to deal with potentially violent situations. Appropriate training for workplace violence can take many forms and can be sourced internally or externally. The aim of this chapter is to help managers understand the processes for identifying training needs and how an appropriate solution should be developed, implemented, and monitored – thus enabling managers to recognise the processes rather than equip them with a complete set of answers.

The chapter also identifies the relative strengths and weaknesses of internally and externally delivered training, so that managers can make an informed choice between the two. Whichever option is chosen, this chapter helps to emphasise that training needs to be specifically designed to meet an individual organisation's needs, so that best value is achieved.

A training development model

7.2   A well designed training or development activity is developed through a three-stage process:

1.   Training Needs Analysis.

2.   Training design, development and testing.

3.   Implementing, monitoring and evaluation.

Each stage of this model is essential to the development of an effective training solution and should be evident in any training programme being offered whether that be internal or external. This chapter will go on to examine each element of the model in detail.

Training Needs Analysis

7.3   The first step in a Training Needs Analysis is to identify the gap between how things are now and how things ought to be. It can apply specifically to the needs of an individual employee or more generally to a job role.

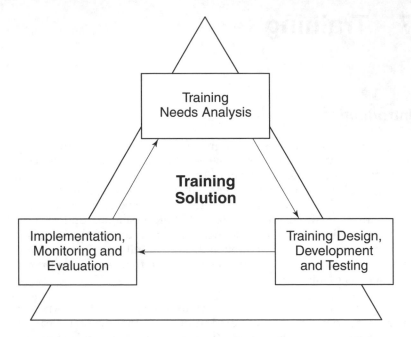

Figure 7.1: General training and development model

Any training or development solution should begin by asking two questions:

1. How has the need for the proposed training been identified?

2. What are the intended learning outcomes of the proposed training?

Identifying the need

7.4 The variety of ways that a training need can be identified are shown in figure 7.2 (below).

A complete review of the risk of conflict and workplace violence across an organisation will identify a range of needs (see CHAPTER 5). Amongst these will be specific training and development requirements for staff performing specific roles and for line managers who are responsible for reducing risk and managing the issues that result from workplace incidents.

A well-designed system for reporting and monitoring incidents of violence in the workplace will automatically provide a continuous needs analysis which will feed directly into the loop of the Training and Development Model. The system will also show internal trends and

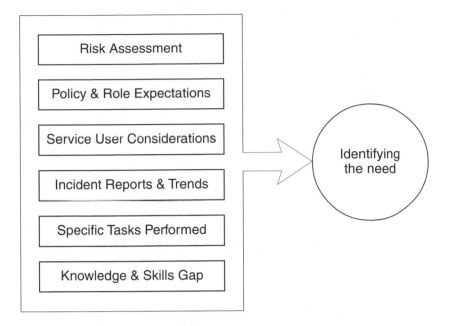

Figure 7.2: Identifying the need

provide information about specific levels of risk, locations, types of incidents, and causes – all of which will help to target the training responses to specific areas of need.

Sector-professional bodies will also provide useful information about trends and initiatives taking place, which might need a training response.

Defining the learning outcomes

7.5　This is an especially important phase of the process. A solution cannot be designed until the specific required outcomes of the proposed training are identified and stated. The outcomes should link directly to the identified needs. The outcome will describe what the objective is for people to achieve and do after they have attended the programme. A good way to start is by saying: 'At the end of the training the delegates will ... ' – and then describe the outcome.

Here is a simple example. A management review has shown that the workplace violence reporting form is not being filled in correctly in 80% of cases. A training need has been identified. The training outcome will be: 'At the end of the training the delegates will be able to correctly complete the reporting form.'

The above example also highlights the importance of ensuring that the need is correctly identified – in this case it may well be that the form is ambiguous, unclear or difficult to follow.

The desired outcomes of the proposed training are an important starting point for the design of the solution to the identified training need.

A simple checklist for the identification of training needs and the development of learning outcomes is given at **7.7**.

Case study

7.6

Ambulance Partnership Against Violence Project

Training Needs Analysis

Until recently training for emergency ambulance staff in the management of violence has been sporadic and very little has been tailored to respond to their unique role and tasks performed. The Partnership therefore undertook a comprehensive analysis of the training needs of emergency crews which involved:

- Analysis of the risks faced.

- Analysis of reported violent incidents.

- Staff perceptions and opinions.

- Analysis of existing training in related subjects.

More than 300 staff were involved and the detailed information that resulted allowed training to be designed to address the specific tasks and challenges faced by emergency crews. The research and consultation identified key training scenarios that staff needed to explore and simple ways of reducing risks on a day to day basis such as when approaching or escorting patients. Subsequent staff feedback on training in London, Wales, Berkshire and West Yorkshire acknowledged the high relevance of all aspects of the programme. The relevance and realism of the programme has been further strengthened by the use of an ambulance for part of the training.

The research also highlighted the key support role of control centre staff despatching crews and of supervisors and managers in supporting staff following a violent incident. Specific training has therefore been designed for these staff groups.

Conclusions

This case study highlights the importance of undertaking a violence-specific Training Needs Analysis. This process will help an organisation to:

- Better understand the problems and risks faced by staff.

- Involve staff in solving problems and developing a training solution.

- Achieve commitment to the training initiative through effective consultation.

- Identify highly relevant training scenarios.

- Come up with safer methods of approaching day to day practices.

- Establish realistic training outcomes and ways of measuring them.

- Protect against criticism or litigation by adopting a rigorous analysis of needs.

- Prevent waste of resources on ineffective or unnecessary training.

Checklist

7.7

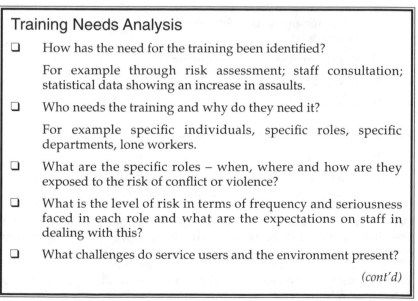

Training Needs Analysis

❑ How has the need for the training been identified?

For example through risk assessment; staff consultation; statistical data showing an increase in assaults.

❑ Who needs the training and why do they need it?

For example specific individuals, specific roles, specific departments, lone workers.

❑ What are the specific roles – when, where and how are they exposed to the risk of conflict or violence?

❑ What is the level of risk in terms of frequency and seriousness faced in each role and what are the expectations on staff in dealing with this?

❑ What challenges do service users and the environment present?

(cont'd)

❏ What statistical data is available to help in the analysis of the risk?

For example data from a reporting system on types of assaults, times of day, locations.

❏ What research is required to investigate and pinpoint the specific issues relating to each role?

For example interviews, focus groups.

❏ Learning outcomes

For example what should each employee be able to understand, appreciate, do or do differently at the end of the proposed training?

Training design, development and testing

7.8   This is the process through which the specification for the learning is created. The aims, objectives and outcomes of the training should be clearly identified from the desired learning outcomes. Decisions then need to be made about the learning methodologies to be used and the models, tutorials, activities and assessment criteria required to match the specification.

The design of a learning activity, course or programme is a specialist task and should be undertaken by the chosen training provider (this may be internal or external – see **7.23**). It is essential to work closely with them to ensure that the design meets all the requirements. The provider needs to know the parameters:

● What is reasonable within the budget?

● Timescales and circumstances.

● What facilities are available?

They also need to know about the target audience:

● What do they already know about the subject?

● What will be the best way of delivering training to them eg in a classroom or through coaching in the workplace?

Generic and 'off the shelf' courses are unlikely to meet the needs of staff working in different roles and who have different problems and concerns.

Training can be delivered in a variety of ways. Traditional methods of delivering training are predominantly in a classroom setting. However, the technology available today has considerably widened the scope for delivering training. Advantage can be taken of for instance distance learning, pre-course workbooks, video, audio and computer-based learning, and virtual classrooms as well as traditional classrooms, workshop and workplace-based learning such as coaching and mentoring. This choice can be somewhat bewildering and it must be recognised that not all of these methods suit everybody's learning needs. Distance learning, for example, can be attractive as a cheap alternative to other methods but it may fail in other important areas. Distance learning is therefore unlikely to be effective other than as a support element to a training programme in the management of violence. Training video's are widely available and although these can provide a useful discussion tool, they will not develop skills and confidence in dealing with violence unless part of a practical training programme.

KUSAB – three areas of learning

7.9

The types of learning an organisation may want to achieve can be broken down into three areas:

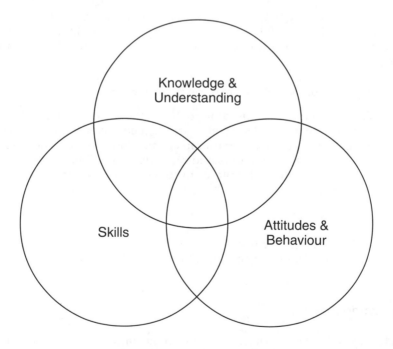

Figure 7.3: The KUSAB Model

- Knowledge and understanding

  This area is generally concerned with things that need to be remembered and understood eg legislation, procedures, theories and models.

- Skills

  This is concerned with practical skills required to become effective such as non-verbal communication, listening, and questioning.

- Attitudes and values

  This area is concerned with matters such as belief, emotions, prejudices and ways of seeing the world eg the perception of someone who uses abusive language or who comes from a different background.

Integration of the learning areas

7.10   Whilst the types of learning have been separated out in **7.9**, most learning activities will have an element of each area within them. Take, for example, some of the elements of conflict management in the workplace. To be effective an individual requires an understanding of the physical and psychological responses people have to feeling threatened (knowledge and understanding), the appropriate skills in listening and non-verbal calming (skills), and the ability to exert self-control and demonstrate the right attitudes towards the other person (attitudes and behaviour).

The integration of these three areas can be achieved in two ways:

1. The methodologies used to deliver the learning need to be appropriate for the area of learning being developed. Several methods can be used – for example, a pre-course workbook to gain the knowledge and understanding, a classroom-based course and coaching in the workplace to develop skills, attitudes and behaviour.

2. The trainer or facilitator can use a variety of methods during a course – for example a taught input on the knowledge and understanding, role-play or practical scenarios to develop skills and a group discussion to develop attitudes and behaviour.

Learning design

7.11   Table 7.1 below shows the three areas of learning and the most appropriate methods of delivering that learning.

	Learning Methodology			
Area of Learning	*Classroom*	*Workshop*	*Distance Learning*	*Workplace*
Knowledge and understanding	XXX	XXX	XXXX	XXX
Skills	XXXX	XXX	XX	XXXX
Attitudes and behaviour	XXXX	XXX	XX	XXXX

XX   Least suited – ineffective or not cost effective.
XXX   Appropriate – but not the most suitable.
XXXX   Best fit – effective and cost effective.

Table 7.1: Selecting the most appropriate learning methodology

The above table illustrates, for example, that properly supported distance learning can be a cost-effective way of providing learning in the area of knowledge and understanding. However, the method is not appropriate for developing the skills or attitudes and behaviours required to manage conflict situations.

Good training design will utilise a range of different methodologies and learning activities to maintain interest, and to meet the different needs of the delegates and the areas of learning. A course in which the trainer spends most of his or her time delivering information to the delegates from the front of the classroom will do little to develop their skills, attitudes or behaviour. Dealing with conflict and violence is very difficult in reality, and if training is to build confidence in the delegates then it needs to be realistic and involve lots or participation. The provider should be able to show how each learning activity will lead to the desired learning outcomes for all the delegates.

Case study

7.12

Hamish Allan Centre, Glasgow City Council

Training design

CHAPTER 4 looked at the review of violence undertaken at the Hamish Allan Centre. An assessment of training needs formed part of the comprehensive review and this provided the basis for the training design process.

(cont'd)

Staff worked in a clearly challenging environment with clients who found themselves in difficult life circumstances. The potential for violence was clear and staff needed to develop their ability to support clients whilst learning to reduce risk and manage chaotic behaviour.

The way in which Glasgow City Council provided services to the homeless was undergoing radical change and it was important that the new training programme contributed to this shift. Staff understandably felt that their workplace presented a unique set of challenges and it was decided that the training would be delivered in part of a hostel where they could problem solve in real living and recreational areas.

The training responded to the risks identified within the review and balanced 'soft' communication skills with those needed to deal with a high-risk incident. The training examined attitudes towards clients and developed greater empathy between staff working in different areas of the system, reducing the potential for internal conflict. The programme gained further credibility when senior managers trained on the first course.

The Centre has recognised the need to reinforce the key training messages in the workplace and to sustain the progress made. Local managers are regularly facilitating feedback, maintaining awareness and involving staff in problem solving. Additional learning needs are being identified and will be incorporated in refresher training.

Conclusions

Some learning points can apply across many sectors:

- It is easy to design an effective training solution given thorough research and understanding of the problem and the learning needs.

- Involving staff in research and design will secure their support for change.

- Wherever possible, provide training in the workplace, and deal with real problems faced by staff.

- Facilitate empathy, teamwork, and effective internal communications.

- Demonstrate commitment and leadership by managers personally participating in the training.

- Look beyond the training to how learning can be reinforced and complacency avoided.

Soft skills and physical intervention training

7.13   The Training Needs Analysis will identify specific training needs which will involve a mixture of knowledge, skills, attitudes and behaviours. Managing conflict demands a unique set of skills which fall into two distinct areas:

1.   Soft skills; and

2.   Physical intervention skills.

The term 'soft skills' in this area is used to identify a range of verbal and non-verbal communication skills that can be used to calm and control the majority of situations.

Physical intervention skills are used when it is necessary to engage in physical contact with another person, who may for example be attacking an individual or a colleague. These can also be divided into two types – interventions that are used in self-protection to disengage or 'break away' from an assailant; and interventions that are used to hold and restrain another person.

Whenever physical skills are taught, practised, and applied for real, there is a risk of injury to everybody involved, and a possibility of either criminal or civil litigation. By selecting an appropriate physical intervention system this risk can be reduced.

Approaches to physical intervention vary greatly. Some self-protection systems include strikes, whilst others are based on non-aggressive techniques. Some systems for holding/ restraining people involve applying locks to joints in order to gain compliance others do not involve any locks or pain. Most organisations requiring physical intervention training are well advised to opt for an effective non-aggressive system, as this will reduce the likelihood of an escalation and the risk of injury to both staff and the assailant.

In some areas of work violence is non-intentional, for example that related to a clinical or mental condition, or a response to treatment. Staff often fail to report such assaults as they accept that the person was confused and couldn't help it. It is important however that organisations encourage the reporting of non-intentional assault, and also teach staff how to avoid it.

Staff need to practice physical interventions if they are to be able to recall and apply them effectively in violent situations. Over a period of time, an individual's level of skills will reduce and it is therefore necessary to provide refresher training – typically every 12–18 months dependant on the complexity and frequency of use of the skills (skills that are rarely used will reduce more quickly).

It is very important that physical intervention techniques are effective, appropriate, properly risk assessed, and are medically and legally defensible. A medical review of each technique will indicate the expected medical implications from its use, and this will assist staff in making a reasonable response in law.

It is also important to be able to justify the inclusion of physical interventions through a rigorous risk assessment and Training Needs Analysis, because there is always an element of injury risk whenever such skills are taught and practised. Employers also need to be prepared for a scenario whereby an employee refuses to participate or is deemed unfit to participate. If the need for such training has been evidenced and documented, managers can support subsequent action that could in certain circumstances include the removal of the employee from duties where the risk exists. This scenario reinforces the need to involve staff representatives and, where appropriate, unions in the training needs identification and design process.

Although the use of physical intervention is a sensitive issue, employers need to face up to it and justify why they do or do not teach such skills, as they could easily find themselves scrutinised either way.

Case study

British Institute of Innkeeping (BII): Physical intervention training

The National Steering Committee on Door Supervision charged the BII with the design and co-ordination of the new National Certificate for Door Supervisors – Licensed Premises (NCDS – LP). The Committee wanted the training to be comprehensive and to make a real contribution to raising standards in an area of work that suffered a poor image.

A comprehensive consultation process had taken place and the Committee accepted the fact that conflict management and physical intervention training was a requirement in this often high-risk work. The Committee also recognised the importance and sensitivity of this type of training and went to considerable lengths to identify a training approach that balanced interpersonal skills, risk reduction and effective non-aggressive physical skills.

Door supervisors attending the training develop a range of non-aggressive physical alternatives to their existing skill bases, and most importantly learn new strategies to reduce conflict and operate within the law. The NCDS – LP is delivered through BII approved training centres and door supervisors are given a 'passport' that shows the elements of training completed. Door supervisors may be required to show a completed passport before being allowed to operate in some local authority areas.

Conclusions

- The importance of thorough consultation is reinforced by this scheme. It has helped to ensure:

  ○ Industry and local authority commitment.

  ○ Relevance of the training solution to the role.

  ○ Credibility and successful accreditation.

- Employers need to acknowledge the fact that physical intervention training is required in some roles. Security providers, purchasers and sector bodies often avoid this issue, possibly because they are unsure how to approach it. In reality many workers are left to use possibly limited and inappropriate physical interventions they have at their disposal – placing everybody at risk. It is better to teach an appropriate set of physical skills needed in the role, together with an understanding of their legal and medical implications. All physical intervention training must be supported by the 'soft skills' that help staff to reduce risk and defuse conflict.

Core content – soft skills

7.14 The Training Needs Analysis should identify the learning needs of people who perform the role or roles being analysed. In general the following constitutes what might be regarded as the core ingredients of any training solution which is intended to meet soft skill needs.

- Organisational policy and values

  A training event is a golden opportunity to reinforce the core values which underpin the organisation's approach to dealing with their clients or customers but within the context of keeping staff safe. There should be greater clarity about the policy and what the organisation expects people to do, and not to do.

- Definitions of workplace violence

  This should clearly outline what the organisation defines as 'violence' and what type of incidents should be considered for reporting. The Health and Safety Executive's (HSE) definition of violence is valuable here.

- Risk assessment

  Employees need to be able to identify risks to their personal safety in the context of workplace violence. They should be able to proactively assess a situation or incident so that they can make an informed assessment of the risk and the consequent action they can take.

- Risk reduction and safety systems

  Employees should be familiar with a safe working practice, security procedures, the location, testing and use of alarms, panic buttons and CCTV equipment.

- Theoretical models of aggression, violence and conflict management

  Understanding the physiological and psychological processes that occur when people become angry, frightened or aggressive can help someone to understand the situation they are in and what may be confronting them.

- Triggers and escalation

  Employees need to be able to recognise the triggers and signs of increasing aggression so that they can anticipate and defuse situations before they become more serious.

- Verbal and non-verbal communication skills

  Employees need to understand the major role of communication and personal space in responding to aggressive situations and practise the specific skills that will help them to manage expectations and deal with challenging behaviour.

- Special groups of people

  Drugs, alcohol, mental illness, learning disabilities, cultural differences and the elderly are some examples of the different challenges that can be presented in the context of workplace violence. Training should include the special needs identified for the sector concerned.

- De-escalation and calming skills and exit strategies

  Employees need to be able to understand the theory and practice of de-escalation and calming through empathy, problem solving and win-win thinking. They also need strategies for getting out of difficult situations when other courses of action are failing.

- Legal issues, self-defence and use of force

  Employees need to have a clear understanding of their rights and responsibilities when confronted with aggressive and violent behaviour. Some organisations have a clear code of practice for dealing with a range of situations. These will vary across sectors and organisations – although everyone has a right to defend themselves or other people from attack. Employees need to have a clear understanding as to the type of circumstance to which this applies.

- Support for staff – post-incident

  Employees need to know what support they can expect and what is available through the organisation from line manger support to specialist counselling.

- Post-incident reporting and debriefing

  The correct reporting of incidents is vital for a number of reasons including statistical information and the need to accurately record the incident in terms which will provide good evidence should the incident go to the courts. Employees need to understand how to properly report an incident and be aware of the reasons why it this is important.

Core content – physical intervention skills

7.15   It is more difficult to identify a core content for physical skills as it will vary a great deal across different sectors. The Training Needs Analysis and risk assessment will identify whether there is a specific need for physical intervention in a particular role. It will also show the most common types of assault, for example whether staff are likely to be hit or grabbed. There is no point in teaching several techniques for getting out of a 'bear hug', if this type of assault is not likely. It is also important to keep the amount of physical interventions taught to a minimum and to develop confidence and competence in these. The more skills that are taught, the less likely staff are to recall them in a stressful situation.

The following are the key pre-requisites to physical skills training:

- Core soft skills

  The core content described for soft skills should be regarded as an essential pre-requisite of any course involving physical intervention skills. Alternatively an integrated course can combine these soft skills with physical intervention training.

- Skills for protecting oneself or another from unlawful assault

  These can comprise skills to protect against strikes and skills to release holds and remove oneself or another from danger. These skills are commonly referred to as 'breakaway' or ' disengagement' techniques. Approaches vary greatly from soft approaches to aggressive systems involving strikes.

- Interventions that are used to hold and restrain another person

  This is often referred to as 'control and restraint' or 'holding skills' and such interventions are normally used to prevent someone from escaping lawful arrest or detention, or preventing them harming themselves or others. Where there is a risk of non-intentional violence such as in some areas of healthcare, staff need to be taught how to avoid this, and how to control the patient or service user in a appropriate and safe manner.

- Legal issues

  Physical intervention carries with it a greater responsibility in that the employees must be critically aware of their powers in relation to detaining someone and the appropriate parts of the law that provide those powers.

Additional physical skills can be added to these core areas, including safer approaches to day to day tasks such as escorting or guiding.

Specialist skills can also be added to the highest-level training such as the use of handcuffs or containing equipment such as the emergency response belt (ERB).

Training duration

7.16 The duration of a training event will vary greatly and depend primarily on the outcomes that are sought and the depth and complexity of the content. In some sectors employees are given pre-set levels of training based upon their role and the risks present, for example:

Level	Desired outcome of training	Duration of training
Level 1	Personal safety awareness and conflict management training.	Typically 1 day duration.
Level 2	Level 1 content plus 'breakaway' skills that can include how to protect oneself or others against attack and to disengage from an assailant.	Typically 2 days' duration.
Level 3	Level 1 and Level 2 content plus skills for holding and restraining individuals.	Typically 2–4 days' duration.

Table 7.2: Training duration

It is important not to fix the duration of courses before actually establishing the need, scope and objectives to be met. Some managers place unrealistic time restrictions on training and some providers will promise the world in a half-day programme. As tempting as this may be in terms of cost and staff release, the training will necessarily be of low quality.

As an example of how course duration can differ; if the need is simply to raise awareness of personal safety issues for a group of workers, this could in some circumstances be done over a half-day. If however the training is intended to develop skills and confidence in actually dealing with challenging behaviour and violent incidents, it could take between one and to two days. The time needed to train 'breakaway and holding skills' also differs greatly as these can range from a few simple principles and skills to comprehensive programmes that cover many potential scenarios. The extent of this training will depend upon the risk assessment, and the nature of the job role, environment and service users – and all these factors will all have a significant influence on the extent of the skills required.

Reviewing the training content

7.17   It is important at this stage to ensure that the solution will satisfy three basic criteria:

1.   Relevance

Is the training content based upon a thorough Training Needs Analysis that considers the role and tasks performed and the risks associated with these? Does the training deliver the intended outcomes, and is it directly relevant to the roles performed and needs of the delegates?

2.   Legal review

Is the content of the course legally correct? Will it stand up to examination in legal proceedings if tested?

3.   Medical review

Additional questions need to be asked when physical interventions are taught: are the learning methods and content safe? Will this stand up to examination in legal proceedings if tested?

The training received by an individual is commonly scrutinised in any legal proceedings. Such proceedings can arise from an incident that has occurred in the workplace, or from an injury sustained during the course of the training itself.

The legal and medical basis for the training provided is often challenged and it is important that the organisation is confident that the training being provided will stand up to such scrutiny should it ever become necessary.

It is the responsibility of the training provider to show the appropriate legal and medical basis that underpins the learning solution being designed. Some providers of physical intervention training have tried to legitimise their approach by adopting police or 'Home Office approved' techniques. This should trigger alarm bells for two reasons; firstly, neither the police nor the Home Office is likely to have approved techniques for use outside of their own organisations and, secondly, police 'officer safety' techniques are not appropriate in the majority of workplaces.

Similar concerns should also arise when providers boast 'special forces' or martial arts credentials, as these are rarely relevant and can indicate an unhealthy focus on 'physical' responses to violence.

Testing the solution

7.18   Before implementing the course or programme, it is a good idea to test it out using a pilot course or courses. The delegates for the pilot course should be from the group for whom the course has been designed and they should be aware that they are taking part in a pilot so that they can provide feedback about the course. It is a good idea to share the course outcomes with them so that they can be fully aware of the intended learning.

The pilot course or courses should be delivered under the same conditions that the fully implemented course will be delivered.

Feedback about the programme should be sought from delegates. This should be gathered by de-briefing the pilot course as soon as possible after the event. It can be achieved through a combination of a group discussion, questionnaires and structured interviews.

The results should be analysed and fed back into the design so that adjustments can be made in the light of the feedback received.

Implementation

7.19   How the programme is implemented will depend very much upon the structure and needs of the particular organisation.

It is important to ensure a good communication strategy is in place so that everyone who needs to know is aware of the training programme, its intended outcomes and value to the organisation. Backing from senior people within the organisation is vital to underline the importance of combating workplace violence and their endorsement should be highly visible.

The programme is likely to be better received if employees have been actively consulted and involved in the Training Needs Analysis research and in the design process.

The rollout of the programme needs consideration, with some thought about who should receive training first. For example, line managers often have to deal with conflict themselves and also have to manage people who have been involved in difficult incidents. Additionally, they are the key people in the processes of incident reporting and after-care. This has to be balanced against the needs of the front line personnel who have to deal with the difficult issues. There are no hard and fast rules but it is important to develop a cohesive, prioritised strategy for implementation.

Once the training has been prioritised in terms of rollout it is important that a training plan is drawn up with time lines. This plan is key to demonstrating commitment to the training over a reasonable time frame, and may be required to satisfy HSE inspectors or other professionals involved in litigation.

It is important that managers and staff are clear as to whether the training offered is mandatory or merely desirable. If it is mandatory – as would normally be the case – the consequences of non-attendance must be established by management and understood by all employees.

The following case studies highlight the different approaches that can be taken to implementing training in large organisations that have diverse needs.

North West London Hospitals NHS Trust

This large NHS Trust incorporates the Central Middlesex and Northwick Park Hospitals. As in other trusts, violence towards staff is real concern within the Trust and the challenge lay in balancing the practicalities of a training rollout with meeting the specific needs of staff in different roles and areas of work.

The Trust therefore uses external specialists to conduct a management review of the higher risk or more specialised areas of the Trust. This identifies key risks and conflict reduction measures and also identifies the specific training requirements. An appropriate unit/ role specific training response is then designed and delivered.

Staff operating in more general areas attend the regular 'open' courses which are geared either towards lone workers or hospital-based staff.

The London Borough of Havering

This large London Borough has a number of directorates, each with very different training needs. The Council has managed to provide a consistent core of training in managing aggression and violence whilst at the same time giving the flexibility to tailor this to meet the different needs of each directorate and work group.

In practice the preferred external provider is put directly in touch with the directorate or part thereof requiring training. The training course is

(cont'd)

---

then tailored through consultation with managers and front line staff. The benefit of this approach is that the authority can be satisfied that the training delivered across the directorates is to a consistent high quality, and the directorates help to shape it to meet the specific needs of their staff and service users. Effective risk assessment needs to underpin this process.

South West Trains

Violence towards staff on the railways is commonplace and South West Trains has made a substantial commitment to staff training in personal safety and in developing customer service skills. The company has developed a range of training programmes that respond to the needs of staff in different roles, and also for managers in recognition of their key support role.

Comprehensive training is now delivered during initial training with regard to personal safety and the management of conflict. Managers also receive training in how to deal with conflict and in the key part they can play in supporting staff following an incident. Individual courses have been designed specifically for:

- Revenue protection.
- Guards and commercial guards.
- Rail operators (station based staff).
- Travel Safe Officers.
- Managers.

This approach ensures that training is focused on the specific role and tasks performed. Other train operating companies have taken innovative approaches including:

Connex South Eastern recognised that although train drivers are less at risk of violence than other on-train staff, there have been occasions where they have been targets. The company therefore provided driver safety managers with training in the delivery of a specific briefing pack for drivers. A guidance booklet supported this.

Thames Trains and Thameslink provide comprehensive staff training in this area, some of which is role-specific and some that is in the form of open access programmes. Although it can be difficult to meet everybody's needs on an open programme, a benefit has been having staff appreciate the roles of other colleagues and to work as part of a wider team.

A major retailer

The retail sector faces a growing problem of violence towards staff and this is often connected with the apprehension of thieves. One retail group provides a dedicated personal safety and conflict management training programme to its security and loss prevention professionals.

The organisation provides clear messages as to the expectations of staff in violent situations in an effort to ensure the safety of everyone. The training also encourages these key managers to brief store colleagues on personal safety issues relating to each specific role, and to encourage vigilance and team work. Before attending the training, delegates are tasked with consulting colleagues in their particular store to identify key issues concerning conflict and violence in their workplace.

A challenge with any training is to ensure the transfer of the skills learnt to the workplace. The organisation has addressed this by involving area managers at the training events, who assist the store representatives in developing a specific action plan for their store. The area managers then follow this up during subsequent store visits.

Brighton Buses

Brighton Buses have responded to concerns over violence towards drivers by providing training in how to reduce risk and deal with difficult behaviour and potentially hostile situations. The company has also developed a response team that will drive out and support drivers who find themselves in such situations. The response team is trained to a higher level, however the same core skills are taught to everyone to ensure a consistent approach and effective teamwork.

Checklist

7.20

Design and Implementation

❑   What are the aims and objectives of the training programme?

❑   How does the content of the programme achieve the aims and objectives?

❑   What areas of knowledge and understanding are required?

(cont'd)

For example, theory, models, legislation, policies and procedures.

❑ What skills are needed by staff?

For example, skills in communication, problem solving, disengagement, escorting, restraint, detaining.

❑ What are the appropriate attitudes and behaviours required?

For example, avoiding physical contact, assertiveness.

❑ What learning methodologies are being used to achieve the development and how appropriate are they to these circumstances?

For example, distance learning, group discussion, practical role play, practice physical skills.

❑ Has the training been tailored to the role and tasks performed?

❑ Have staff been consulted in the design process?

❑ Can any of the training be delivered in the workplace and include discussion on realistic situations and include problem solving opportunities?

❑ How is the content reviewed to ensure it is tactically effective, legally correct and medically safe?

❑ How will the programme be piloted and who should take part in the pilot?

❑ How will the pilot be evaluated?

❑ Who needs to know about the programme and how will it be communicated?

❑ What backing and support (and from whom) is available at senior level?

❑ How will the programme be rolled out? Who will receive it first – or will it be a mixed rollout? Can some groups, roles, individuals be trained together?

Monitoring and evaluating the solution

7.21 There are several reasons why the programme should be evaluated.

● At the very basic level, the quality of the actual training event or activity should be evaluated to see if it is delivering what it was designed to deliver and feedback should be sought so that it can be improved or modified.

● The next level of evaluation informs about the effectiveness of the development activity on individual performance.

- Finally, the effectiveness of the activity can be measured in terms of impact upon the organisation. For example reduction in assaults, the number of reported incidents, quality of reporting and/ or improved handling of incidents may all indicate better performance overall in dealing with issues of personal safety.

The monitoring and evaluation of the programme needs to fit with the existing infrastructure of the organisation. There may already be a well-developed training and development process in place which incorporates an evaluation process that operates at the three levels mentioned. If a good reporting system is in place it will provide data which will directly feed back information to help in evaluating the effectiveness of the training.

Figure 7.4 (below) shows a typical process that combines the individual development needs of the delegate with the feedback required to monitor and evaluate the programme. From an individual point of view, the delegate should define his or her personal learning objectives before the course, preferably involving his or her line manager. A short time after the course they should review the objectives and establish the learning outcomes achieved.

From an organisational point of view, delegates can complete an immediate post-course evaluation, which will establish reactions to, and satisfaction with, the programme. About four to six weeks later, delegates should provide further feedback about the impact that the programme has had in they way they perform in the workplace. This is then fed into the process of Training Needs Analysis and design for continuous improvements to the programme.

It is worth mentioning here some of the inherent difficulties with evaluation that an organiser should be aware of. Evaluating the success of a programme in terms of acquiring knowledge is fairly easy to achieve through a test or exam. Physical skills are a little more difficult to assess – it requires time to practise and then the learner should be able to demonstrate his or her mastery of the skill. The most difficult area is that of attitude and behavioural change which is a longer process and more difficult to measure objectively. In fact, the most effective, short term, way is to accept a subjective judgement from the delegate eg 'Do you now feel more confident about dealing with conflict than you did before the course?'

Training is usually only one small part of the whole solution to the issues of conflict and workplace violence, and the direct correlation between 'cause' and 'effect' is hard to isolate. The number of reported incidents has increased – but is this because the problem is getting worse, or because the training programme is educating the delegates, or because the form has been redesigned to make it easier to fill in?

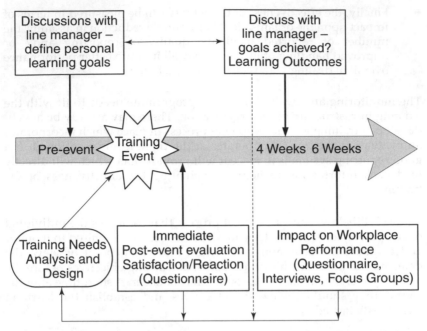

Figure 7.4: A typical delegate feedback process combining individual and organisational needs

---

Case study

London Borough of Croydon: Parking Services

Parking Services staff performing various roles can face abuse on a regular basis. The London Borough of Croydon recognised the importance of delivering high quality training to staff and also in evaluating the effectiveness of this training in the workplace.

The workplace evaluation was undertaken three months post-training and was based primarily on a questionnaire. Key questions asked included:

Since attending the course:	Yes	No
Are you more confident in dealing with conflict situations?	87%	13%
Do you feel better able to reduce risk?	97%	3%
Do you feel better equipped to manage customer expectations?	90%	10%
Have you been involved in a conflict situation?	29%	71%

(cont'd)

Those that had been in a conflict situation since the training were asked if they were able to use any aspects of the training – and if so what?

Respondents stated that they had utilised their increased awareness of positioning and escape routes and also their verbal and non-verbal calming skills.

Participants were also asked which of parts of the training had proved most beneficial, and responses indicated that the content had been directly relevant to the job.

The Glasgow City Centre Hamish Allen Centre undertook a similar workplace evaluation with equally positive feedback.

Summary

7.22 Ideally the adoption of a qualitative approach will be supported by high quality quantitative data on incidents, complaints etc. An effective reporting and monitoring system will therefore play a key part in workplace evaluation.

Staff perceptions and opinions count, and the fact that staff feel safer and more confident is a valid indicator. Independent facilitators can also gather this information through structured interviews and focus groups. If a questionnaire is used, ways of encouraging staff to complete and return it need to be identified, whilst ensuring the integrity of the process.

The complete process of training and development in relation to the issues of workplace violence is summarised in figure 7.5 (below).

Internal or external training providers

7.23 The decision about whether to use an internal training department or an external training provider is quite a difficult one and needs some careful consideration. There are pros and cons to each and they need to be weighed properly to ensure the decision is the right one for the organisation.

Internal provider

7.24 The most compelling reason for choosing an internal training department is usually cost. Even if some form of internal cross-charging

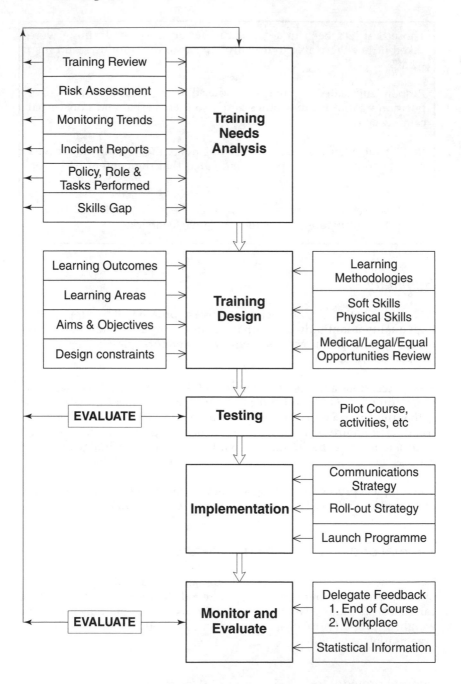

**Figure 7.5: A summary of the training and development process
for workplace violence**

is used, the visible cost of the training will inevitably be considerably less than using an external provider and it is difficult to make any direct comparison between the two. If the budget is the paramount consideration, it can be quite difficult to justify the use of an external provider.

However, the 'visible costs' do not always tell the whole story. An internal training department will generally be aligned to the needs of the particular business and its training staff will have a great deal of experience of training in their specialism. Usually the issues of workplace violence are a long way down the essential training required to become an effective nurse, social worker or train manager and therefore internal trainers tend to be less informed and skilled in this area. There are costs to be met, therefore, which rarely figure in the visible costs. These will include those of specialist research into the subject of violence in the workplace, design of the programme and specific trainer training necessary to deliver an effective conflict management training programme.

If there is a good system for reporting and analysing incidents of workplace violence the internal provider will be well informed of changing needs and the information required to keep a training programme updated with the current needs of staff will be readily available. This will work well if the training department also has a system for monitoring and evaluating the training that it provides.

If an organisation's workplace violence issues require physical intervention training, then it must be remembered that the risks to the organisation increase with the level of physical intervention required. The internal provider must be able to satisfy managers that the interventions are both appropriate and medically and legally defensible.

Most internal training departments attract 'can do' people who are willing and eager to help and enthusiastic about new challenges. Care is needed to ensure that they can provide training specific to requirements – not what they may think is needed. A number of providers will offer to train trainers and some organisations run 'open access' trainer development programmes on the subject of personal safety. As always, it is important to be clear about the outcomes required so that an accurate assessment of the options can be made. It is unreasonable to expect someone to become either a skilled trainer or a specialist in the management of conflict and violence through attending a three-day course. The most effective internal delivery is likely to result from:

- A thorough violence Training Needs Analysis and training design process.

- Consultation at all levels and testing of the design/s.

- Careful selection of internal trainers.

- A comprehensive bespoke trainer development programme.

- Coaching support from specialists for the new trainers on initial deliveries.

- On-going review, evaluation, trainer support and revalidation.

The management of conflict and violence is a complex and challenging subject to teach, and it is not as straightforward as subjects such as manual handling or first-aid.

Internal provision may be the most practical or cost effective option, but if it is done well – it will not be cheap.

Checklist

Internal provider

❏ How well is the department equipped to do a Training Needs Analysis on the requirements for dealing with workplace violence?

❏ Can they design a properly researched solution that will provide effective development for the employees?

❏ Are the trainers suitably experienced, qualified and credible to provide specialised training in managing conflict and workplace violence?

❏ Does the trainer development programme include coaching and on-going support, or is it a stand-alone programme and un-supported.

❏ Does the Training Needs Analysis indicate a requirement for skills in physical intervention?

❏ How has the training solution been reviewed to ensure that it is tactically appropriate, legally correct and medically safe?

❏ How will the training be monitored and evaluated to ensure it is effective and meeting the current needs of the workplace?

Case study

Servisair: Trainer Development

Airport ground handling specialists Servisair decided to train internal trainers to deliver conflict management training. Servisair recognised the importance of designing a programme based on their unique needs, and brought in conflict management specialists to:

● Help identify the specific learning needs and scenarios.

● Design a training programme for customer facing colleagues.

● Train selected Servisair employees in the delivery of the programme.

The programme was branded 'Managing the Tough Stuff' and focused on staff skills in reducing conflict and in dealing with the emotive and difficult situations that can occur at an airport. The programme was intended to build on existing customer service skills training and to enhance confidence and professionalism in handling the more challenging situations.

Conclusions

Servisair recognised the risks associated with trainer training and took care to ensure that this approach did not dilute the impact of the programme. Key success factors that can be shared with other organisations considering such an approach include:

● Selective use of external specialists in design and trainer development.

● Designing a programme exclusive to Servisair needs.

● Selecting local (airport-based) trainers with operational experience and credibility amongst peers.

● Providing coaching by external specialists on trainer's first deliveries, to give confidence and help ensure a successful launch.

● Producing highly customised and professional support materials to reinforce the value placed on this training.

● Drawing on trainers' experiences at follow-up workshops and continuously seeking to draw and share the learning across the organisation.

External provider

7.25   A good external provider will develop a training solution specific to requirements and deliver it using good quality trainers who are experienced in this area. Spending money on engaging external 'experts' sends a strong message to employees about how seriously the issue is being taken by the organisation.

Generally, external providers will be more expensive in terms of visible costs. This extra investment needs to be justified and the most compelling justification is that the external provider has specialist knowledge, experience and expertise in the field of managing conflict and workplace violence.

Of course, most external providers will claim to have such expertise in abundance. There are many providers ranging from small 'sole trader' companies through to larger organisations who have developed their own 'unique' solution to managing conflict. Some are very good and some are not so good. The difficulty is making the right choice from the plethora of providers who claim to have just the solution being sought.

In simple terms the client will need to find out from the provider if:

- Their solution will equip the individuals at risk with the knowledge, skills, attitudes and behaviour to deal effectively with the incidents of workplace violence they may face.

- Their organisation has processes which ensure the training need is correctly identified, the solution is properly designed, and that there is an evaluation process that provides feedback to validate and improve the product.

- Their training is properly designed to meet specific needs and is sufficiently robust to be medically and legally defensible if required.

- The people used to deliver the training are properly trained and experienced in delivering this type of training and understand the particular problems of the client.

This is a matter of asking the right questions. Providers will obviously present themselves in their best light and will tend to gloss over or leave out the areas where they might be weak. They will also be optimistic about their ability to meet any and all expectations and may make promises which will, in fact, stretch their resources to the limit. Questions, therefore, need to target the areas important to the organisation and the answers should provide factual evidence – not vague assurances or optimistic promises.

A good example is the provider's ability to deliver:

'We need this programme delivering quickly. It will involve 40 one-day courses delivered over a two-month period in four different locations. How will you achieve the delivery schedule?'

'Oh, we'll cope okay. We have a good network of competent trainers. We've never let a customer down yet.'

This is rather vague, the word 'cope' sounds a little worrying, and 'network of trainers' might mean anything. It is important to know how many trainers they will commit to the programme, how they propose to cover all locations, and what will happen if one trainer becomes ill or unable to deliver at short notice.

The checklist below provides a guide to the questions that need to be asked of an external provider to help gauge their ability to meet all requirements. This is not exhaustive and it is important that questions are also asked that are specific to local needs.

Checklist

External providers

❑   What evidence can they provide of their expertise in the field of managing conflict and workplace violence?

❑   What experience do they have in the organisation's specific sector and work?

❑   What do the other organisations they have worked with say about them?

❑   What evidence can they provide as to the effectiveness of their training in the workplace?

❑   What methodology will they use to identify the training needs of the organisation in the area of conflict management and workplace violence?

❑   What learning methods are they proposing to use? Are they practically-based and in line with the training needs identified?

❑   How do they ensure that the content of their programmes is appropriate and legally correct?

❑   How do they ensure that the physical interventions used are medically safe?

❑   How do they conduct their training to ensure the delegates are trained in a safe environment?

❑   How do they develop their trainers?

(cont'd)

❑   What level of resources will they commit to the programme and how will they deal with short-term issues such as a trainer becoming ill?

❑   What level of programme evaluation do they offer and how will it be fed back to the organisation?

❑   Are they likely to provide credible expert witness support if required?

Combining internal and external provision

7.26   Combining the two options can provide a compromise and solution to this problem. It can be achieved by engaging an external provider to undertake a Training Needs Analysis and design a solution. The provider could be asked to deliver training directly to the higher risk and more demanding staff groups, and they could train internal trainers to deliver the bulk of the remaining programmes.

This solution is attractive because the visible costs are kept relatively low and the benefits of using an external provider are achieved to some degree. However, assuming the provider has been carefully chosen, the weak link in the solution lies in the actual internal delivery of the programme.

- The manager should be satisfied that the provider has the additional ability to actually train trainers. Training of trainers is a 'step up' from delivering training and involves the expertise to develop trainers in the knowledge and skills of facilitation, presentation, communication and conflict management.

- Consideration must be given to the ability of internal trainers to deliver to a programme and whether they will have sufficient 'credibility' in the subject to win over the delegates. This is quite an important consideration. It has already been stated that spending money on engaging external 'experts' sends a strong positive message to employees about how seriously the issue is being taken by the organisation. Using internal trainers, who are not seen as experts by the delegates attending the programmes, can seriously dilute this message. New recruits are a much easier audience than experienced staff.

- If the organisation requires training in physical intervention then the risks become greater. The protection against the risk is only as good as the weakest link. A good Training Needs Analysis and a well designed programme can be let down by inexpert delivery.

Case studies

Select Service Partner

Select Service Partner (SSP) recognised the difficult situations and risks employees can face running its UK network of rail station bars and retail outlets. Although the programme is still in its early stages, SSP has developed an innovative approach to the potentially daunting task of training large numbers of staff spread out across the UK.

The solution has comprised involving external specialists on design and strategy, and in the delivery of comprehensive training in risk reduction and conflict management to bar managers. The bar managers are now rolling out key personal safety awareness and conflict avoidance messages to their customer facing staff, with the help of a specially designed training pack.

The whole process is supported by regional 'conflict facilitators' who provide additional support to the bar managers and ensure staff in other retail outlets receive training. The conflict facilitators have undergone specialist training that also equips them to follow up violent incidents, to facilitate support for staff involved, and to draw and share any learning. A key tool for the facilitators is the new violence-specific reporting process that provides quality information on incidents and records the follow-up process. This reporting process is explored in the context of reporting in CHAPTER 5.

Conclusions

SSP has developed what should prove to be a cost effective and pragmatic response to staff support and development in a national, commercial operation. Key learning points from their approach are:

- Clear scope and prioritisation of training based on role performed and potential risks.

- Clear responsibilities and support at local, regional and national level is essential.

- Successful partnership with external providers.

- The value of an effective reporting mechanism that underpins training, staff support and management response.

(cont'd)

Virgin Trains

Virgin Trains were embarking upon a complete replacement of their fleet. This required an extensive training programme across the whole company on all aspects of operating the new trains. It was decided to include conflict management training for all customer facing staff as part of the programme.

Virgin Trains invited an external provider to conduct a review of the conflict management training needs of front line staff and design tailored programmes, which could be included in the role-specific training for each group of staff. They also asked the external provider to provide a trainer training programme for their existing team of trainers which would enhance them in the skills required to facilitate the conflict management aspects of the new programme. The one-week trainer course was supported by a comprehensive training manual, development workshops for all trainers and individual support for trainers who needed additional help. Whilst the trainer training was being conducted, the external provider also delivered a series of the courses they had designed. These were evaluated and amendments made before handing over the programme to the in-house training team.

Conclusions

Virgin Trains wanted to include conflict management training as an integral part of their extensive in-house training but recognised the specialist nature of the subject and the need to develop their training staff in a new set of skills to facilitate the programme. The key success factors recognised are:

- A true partnership developed between the external provider and Virgin Trains. The programme was developed in a way which drew on the 'workplace' expertise of the internal training team and the 'specialist' expertise of the external provider.

- Tailored conflict management content is integral to a general training programme.

- Ongoing support for trainer and programme development is critical. Partnerships must extend to bringing trainers 'up to date' in latest trends, techniques etc.

- Tailored programmes delivered, tested and evaluated by an external provider must fully meet the customer's needs before being handed over for internal delivery.

Checklist

Combine internal and external providers

❏ Can the external provider show evidence to prove it has experience of providing trainer training?

❏ Will the training enable internal trainers to provide the programme in a way that is professional and credible?

❏ What level of ongoing trainer coaching and support is offered?

❏ Does the training require physical interventions? If so, review the decision and be sure the trainers can teach this safely and effectively.

Training the managers

7.27 Managers are often forgotten when it comes to violence management training. The needs of managers, particularly line managers, are two fold.

Firstly, they are often called into disputes involving customers or members of the public which have escalated and become too difficult for the member of staff to deal with. They may have already made the situation worse. Additionally, they are often dealing with situations when things have gone wrong and the potential for conflict is high. Consequently, there is a clear need for line managers in these situations to be personally skilled in conflict resolution as part of their role. They also need to be aware of the techniques and skills in this area provided to the people they manage.

Secondly, they have a vital role to play in the management of incidents of workplace violence and the provision of front line support both during and after the process. They are key players in ensuring that such incidents are properly recorded and reported and that their staff carry out their roles in a way which achieves the organisation's goals in a safe and customer-friendly way. Staff can be affected by incidents in many different ways and need an individual response from their line manager.

The second point above is particularly important. Line managers have a great deal of influence in relation to the approach to dealing with conflict and violence in the workplace. Their individual attitude towards the whole issue will greatly influence how seriously the people who work for them approach the subject. This influence will affect attitudes towards risk assessment, approach to conflict situations, reporting and aftercare. Some people are badly affected by incidents that other members of staff might take in their stride. Sometimes the after effects of an incident do not set in until several hours or several days later and managers need to be aware of and look for the signs which indicate that the incident remains unresolved. The way in which the manager deals with the individual will have an influence upon the speed that he or she will recover from the incident. This is dealt with in more detail in CHAPTER 9.

To ensure effective line manager training, the Training Needs Analysis for the role should encompass both of these areas in relation to conflict management and violence in the workplace.

Case study

Nando's: Manager Development

Nando's has for some years been proactive in creating a safe and welcoming environment for staff and customers in its restaurants. As with other businesses operating in inner city areas, vulnerability to crime is a real issue.

Nando's has focused on developing the awareness and skills of its managers and assistant managers in preventing and responding to conflict and risk situations, and in how to seek and provide support afterwards.

The company's management training programme incorporates a specific two-day input on these issues. For realism the training is delivered at a restaurant and practical scenarios are recreated ranging from dealing with a disgruntled customer to a robbery. Post-incident issues are addressed to raise managers' awareness of trauma support and legal/ reporting requirements.

Nando's has found that carefully designed training increases the range of strategies managers have for dealing with difficult situations, and subsequently enhances professionalism and service delivery.

Conclusions

Many organisations fail to recognise the need to train supervisors and managers in their key role in preventing and dealing with conflict and violence, even though they can be just as vulnerable as their staff. Investment in training managers in these areas can bring the following returns:

- Improved confidence, professionalism and service delivery.

- Reduced risk of crime and personal violence.

- Improved post-incident management.

- Compliance with legislative requirements.

- Positive messages for staff who see managers 'lead by example'.

- Reduced vulnerability to criticism and litigation.

The Institute of Occupational Safety and Health (IOSH) has recognised the needs of managers in this area, and has introduced a specific course within its Professional Development Training Programme on 'Managing work-related violence'. IOSH also offers another course 'Negotiating skills and handling conflict' that focuses on handling 'internal conflicts' within organisations.

8 Incident Management

Introduction

8.1   Earlier chapters within the handbook have rightly focused on preventing violence or at least reducing it. This chapter will focus on the effective management of an incident when it does occur, and how its impact can be reduced. CHAPTER 9 POST-INCIDENT MANAGEMENT will consider the steps that should be taken to support staff following the incident and the lessons that should be learned from what has happened. It will also examine the prosecution process.

Although every eventuality cannot be planned for, this chapter highlights the importance of planning and practising the response to foreseeable incidents. Thankfully, only a small proportion of incidents involving workplace violence develop into serious situations which demand an exceptional response. A thorough risk assessment will identify the likelihood of a serious incident happening within the organisation and this in turn will determine the appropriate preparation that needs to be undertaken for the possibility. It is tempting to define 'serious' in terms of 'injury' to a victim. In the main, this will be an important benchmark but other considerations are important, for example, the impact on service delivery and other service users. Violence and intimidation in an environment like a hospital can seriously disrupt a busy casualty department and cause great anxiety to people who are already feeling quite vulnerable. The risk of serious injury might not be great but the need to deal quickly and decisively with the incident is clear and in this sense it can be regarded as a 'serious' incident.

Airport departure lounges provide an example of a different type of serious situation. Large groups of people who are angry about a flight cancellation can quickly turn into a 'mob' and direct their frustration personally at the two or three front line staff who are trying to deal with the situation. Again, the risk of serious physical injury to them is quite low, but their ability to resolve the problem is limited and there can be long-term risks from being exposed to aggressive personal attacks and being expected to manage perceived 'no win' situations with little support. In the airport scenario there is the added concern that tensions on the ground lead to conflict on the aircraft, which is potentially very serious, and difficult to manage. Rather than expecting staff to 'cope with the situation', the organisation has a responsibility to identify the risk, reduce it, and plan and prepare for such incidents.

Even though events will not always go to plan, the rigour of the planning process will help ensure that the systems are in place and that staff and managers are better prepared to deal with the situations that arise.

It is particularly important to prepare and practise a response to violent incidents because they are often highly chaotic and emotive situations where things can happen quickly and employees will find it difficult to think clearly, rationally and objectively. Some areas can be pre-empted, practised and rehearsed so that they become part of an automatic response, allowing staff more room to effectively assess and respond dynamically to the unfolding threat.

Figure 8.1 (below) reinforces the importance of undertaking a violence risk assessment to establish key risk areas, and putting in place measures to reduce these risks. This process will help identify the key incident scenarios that the organisation can then plan and train for.

Risk assessment and risk reduction have already been covered in earlier chapters, and this section will focus on the key elements of incident management and the vital rehearsal and testing of them.

Some of the aspects of incident management covered here, such as the preserving of evidence, may seem a little over the top for some areas of work. It is important however to prepare for the worst-case scenario, the likelihood of which may be low but the impact devastating.

Key scenarios

8.2   The risk assessment process outlined in CHAPTER 5 RISK ASSESSMENT AND REPORTING will have highlighted key areas of risk and control measures will be put in place to tackle these (see CHAPTER 6 RISK REDUCTION). In preparing for the management of incidents it is important to use the risk assessment findings as the basis for the scenarios to be planned for and practised.

Roles and responsibilities

8.3   Communications can quickly breakdown when emotions are high and people are under pressure. It is important to be clear about roles and responsibilities prior to an incident occurring to avoid any confusion about who is responsible for what. This should include specific job roles for individuals and also the part to be played by the wider team that might be involved. For example, what part will the reception, security, domestic and office staff play when an incident occurs in their area. Who takes control, how are they supported, who calls for help, who takes down descriptions, are all questions that need to be addressed. Everyone needs to be involved and has a part to play – even if it is in the

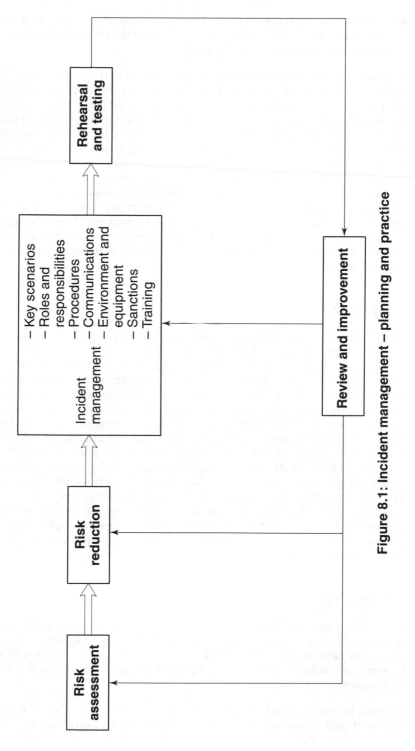

Figure 8.1: Incident management – planning and practice

background. In situations involving lone working, the communications and expectations need to be clear between lone workers and colleagues in the office, control centre or switchboard.

Assumptions about roles need to be questioned and specific roles and responsibilities made explicit. For example, an assumption that the receptionist will call the police in the event of a serious incident – he or she may assume that it is the duty manager who will do so. It is equally important that staff know what they should not do; for example rushing in and possibly escalating the situation, or taking action which might put themselves or other people in danger. Staff can act unpredictably when the adrenaline is flowing and clarity therefore needs to be established as to what they should and should not do before an incident occurs. Many organisations install panic alarms but few offer guidance and training about when to use them and how people should respond. When the alarm is activated in a real situation, the consequence may be that nobody responds because they think someone else will, or everyone rushes in and makes things worse.

Response teams

8.4   Many organisations, especially hospitals, are beginning to operate 'incident response teams'. These are multi-disciplinary teams and follow a similar concept to the 'crash teams' that respond to cardiac arrest. The pro's and con's to this approach need to be carefully considered. Some organisations feel the response team is intrusive and can damage relationships between local staff and patients or service users. This is a legitimate fear and the deployment of an incident response team can be a bit like 'the cavalry' arriving. The team may have little understanding of the situation as it has developed and may take a harder line because they have the numbers to do so, and little empathy with the people involved. On the other hand, vulnerable staff can benefit from the knowledge that they will get competent help quickly. Careful selection of response teams and a high level of training are vital if they are to operate safely and earn the respect of staff. The training should include a strong emphasis upon the soft skills of conflict resolution, as well as appropriate physical intervention techniques.

Leadership

8.5   In common with most situations which are unpredictable, the most critical role in incident management is leadership. Supervisors and managers need to have the confidence and skills to take control of an incident and its immediate aftermath. Staff will look to them for direction and example.

Training in conflict management is often perceived as the preserve of front line staff and managers are rarely included in the staff-training programme. In practice, the managers need conflict resolution skills in their line management role – since they are often brought in to 'sort things out' when the situation between the staff member and the service user has already escalated. Additionally, they need the knowledge and skills to manage an incident and aftermath. Managers who prefer to use a consultative leadership style can find it difficult to adjust from their preferred style to the more directive style required in a crisis. The concept of 'situational leadership' is useful in training, to help managers recognise their preferred style and to understand the need to adapt their style to the situation – staff will want clear direction and decisions when their personal safety depends upon it. Senior management needs to provide clarity about the level of authority given to managers and staff during an incident and how and when decisions should be escalated to a more senior level.

Case study

Select Service Partner

Select Service Partner (SSP) has recently introduced flow charts (see figure 8.2 below) to help supervisors to understand their role and responsibilities should a violent incident occur. At higher risk venues such as licensed bars, SSP managers have also been given comprehensive training in how to prevent and respond to violent incidents. These managers are provided with a specific training pack that helps them to educate their staff about what is required. Flow charts are a useful tool for achieving clarity and an invaluable checklist for managers and staff during an incident and its aftermath, when important things can easily be forgotten.

SSP unit supervisor

8.6   Figure 8.2 (below) outlines the SSP's violence incidents unit supervisor's responsibilities.

Procedures

8.7   The importance of clear communications and role expectations have already been discussed. Communication links, roles and responsibilities, levels of decision making and accountabilities need to be written down in the form of clear guidance and procedures. Flow charts are a useful way of providing the whole picture for and simplifying responsibilities and communication links. A good model exists in most organisations in the fire procedures, and the same approach should be taken with violent incidents.

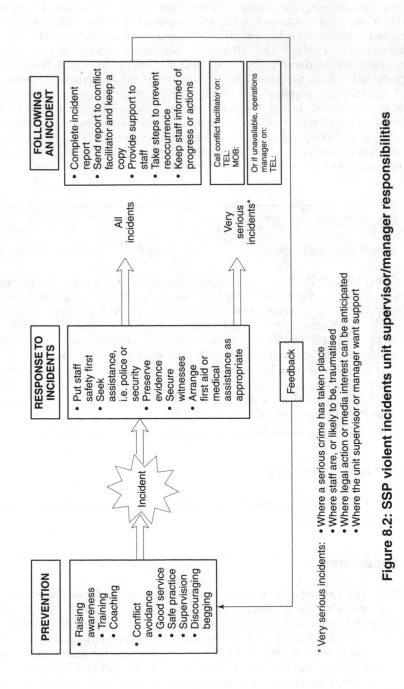

PREVENTION

- Raising awareness
- Training
- Coaching

- Conflict avoidance
- Good service
- Safe practice
- Supervision
- Discouraging begging

Incident

RESPONSE TO INCIDENTS

- Put staff safety first
- Seek assistance, i.e. police or security
- Preserve evidence
- Secure witnesses
- Arrange first aid or medical assistance as appropriate

All incidents

Very serious incidents*

FOLLOWING AN INCIDENT

- Complete incident report
- Send report to conflict facilitator and keep a copy
- Provide support to staff
- Take steps to prevent reoccurrence
- Keep staff informed of progress or actions

Call conflict facilitator on:
TEL:
MOB:

Or if unavailable, operations manager on:
TEL:

Feedback

* Very serious incidents:
- Where a serious crime has taken place
- Where staff are, or likely to be, traumatised
- Where legal action or media interest can be anticipated
- Where the unit supervisor or manager want support

Figure 8.2: SSP violent incidents unit supervisor/manager responsibilities

Preserving evidence

8.8   One key area requiring guidance and procedures is that of preserving evidence.

Violent incidents often result in the prosecution of the perpetrator, a process that will be examined in detail in CHAPTER 9. The success of the prosecution will depend on the quality of the evidence that supports it, and unfortunately cases collapse at court due to simple errors made at the time of the incident in gathering and protecting evidence. Things that may seem trivial at the time, can have a dramatic impact in court as the defence seeks to discredit prosecution evidence.

Rules of disclosure highlight the duty of the prosecution to disclose all evidence, whether it will stand for or against the defendant. Organisations must therefore realise that anything that could be deemed as evidence relating to the case, for example, any incident report forms or records, will form part of the legal process. There are limited exceptions for documents such as medical records, which may not need to be disclosed.

The following basic rules will help to secure and preserve important evidence:

- Securing witnesses

  It is important that when an incident has occurred immediate steps are taken to secure the details of any witnesses. Witnesses could take the form of service users, other customers, unconnected bystanders and staff. Some of these will put themselves forward; others will quickly disappear given any delay and half a chance. Training for managers and staff should recognise and highlight this, and witness details should be required on incident report forms.

- Identification

  Cases can be won and lost on identification evidence. The first description noted of an assailant or other crime suspect, will be regarded as 'best evidence' and will need to be preserved and disclosed in any subsequent prosecution. Staff need to understand this and know what to look for when they see a suspect, particularly any distinctive features or clothing. For example, many people wear brown bomber jackets, but this will be narrowed greatly if a distinctive logo or mark is noted. In serious incidents where the police have become involved, it is important that the investigating officers are given any original notes of descriptions, even if this is the registration number of a vehicle written on the back of a matchbox. If the identification evidence of a witness is to be credible it is important that they are not subject to outside influence. They should not, for example, be shown the CCTV recording as this would impact on any subsequent identification immediately following the incident or at a later stage in an identification parade.

- Closed Circuit Television (CCTV)

  Recordings of an incident often form part of the key evidence. The quality of the system and the way in which it is managed (tape quality for example) will affect the quality of the image recorded, as outlined in CHAPTER 6. Another factor influencing the value of the CCTV evidence is the way it is handled following the incident. In court the defence may seek to discredit the CCTV evidence by casting doubt upon its integrity. Accurate records therefore need to be kept that capture the movements of the recording. Following serious incidents where police are called the tape or disk will ideally be left running until the investigating officer removes it personally from the machine. This has two benefits:

  o   It ensures continuity of evidence thereby removing avenues of doubt.

  o   It records the scene immediately following the incident and therefore reduces speculation about people's actions or possible contamination of the scene (see **8.9** below).

Preserving the scene

8.9   Serious assaults and crimes such as armed robbery will normally involve an immediate police response. Whilst waiting for the police to arrive staff have a key role to play in the immediate preservation of the scene and subsequent evidence. There will be an immediate need to remove further danger and 'contain the area', keeping some people in and others out.

The advances in forensic science and in particular DNA, have increased the importance of particles, fibres and body fluids in evidence. The value of such evidence is severely limited if contamination of forensic evidence occurs and this is most likely to happen immediately after the incident has occurred when the various parties involved are still in an around the scene. This can be done quite unwittingly, for example a supervisor helping to restrain the offender, and then sitting with the victim waiting for the police to arrive. If the incident involved forensic evidence then there may be an issue of cross-contamination of fibres or blood – the supervisor may have transferred them. Movement to or from the scene should also be limited. Human nature makes people curious and incidents attract passers by and sightseers. To preserve evidence in serious cases, the scene should be cordoned off in some way and necessary access should be confined to a specific path which will reduce the likelihood of people treading in evidence.

Covering a weapon or other key item of evidence, by a 'clean' item such as the lid from a photocopy paper box, can protect it. Articles of clothing can provide valuable evidence and should be isolated and protected. Surfaces and objects that could produce fingerprints also need to be protected.

Access to barrier tape and police evidence bags is an important part of preparation for an incident and many nightclubs have police self-sealing bags into which they put confiscated drugs. This scenario is potentially open to abuse and venue managers should ensure that the areas where searches and confiscations commonly take place are covered by CCTV, and that confiscated items are recorded and secured. This also improves continuity of evidence. Staff should conduct searches and seizures in the presence of witnesses (as far as possible those of the same sex as the subject) and in the view of cameras. The searching of people is a sensitive issue and tends to be a condition of access to a building or secure area. It will only be permitted if the individual consents to a search, and it is vital that proper training and procedures are in place to ensure searching is lawful and professional.

Some of these measures may sound extreme and may have more relevance to some workplaces than others. Each incident needs to be treated according to the seriousness of the situation. The response should be reasonable and proportionate in the circumstances.

As with all of the areas outlined in this section clear written procedures and guidance should be in place for searching, confiscating, and preserving evidence. The issue of reporting and prosecution is covered further in CHAPTER 9.

Communications

8.10 Communications with other agencies particularly the police, specialist consultants and the media is another important matter to consider. These issues are addressed in CHAPTER 4 DEVELOPING AND IMPLEMENTING POLICY and it is important to reinforce here the importance of being proactive in responding to media interest following a violent incident. Considerable harm can be done to both the individuals involved and the reputation of the organisation if this is not handled well.

Environment and equipment

8.11 In CHAPTER 6 the aspects of design, layout, security and equipment have been explored in depth as part of a risk reduction strategy. The focus of this section is to discuss how to utilise these effectively when preparing an incident response. For example some organisations fit what are commonly known as 'bandit screens' that are invisible but can be activated in fractions of a second by a staff member at risk. Staff are taught how to activate such devices but are rarely advised on when this should be done. These may seem obvious in an armed robbery, but other incidents are more ambiguous and staff can face a crisis of decision, fearing they may look silly or be criticised for activating the screen or a panic alarm. The ability to assess a dynamic situation (see CHAPTER 5) is essential, and should form part of training. The same point applies to alarms and even a simple issue like calling the police. These decisions can be hard to make when staff are frightened and not thinking clearly.

It is of course vital that alarms and other equipment are regularly checked to avoid problems when they are needed for real. Consultants undertaking reviews regularly find that panic alarms do not work, or cannot easily be accessed. These are frequently disconnected during alterations and improvements to other systems. A mechanism should be in place that ensures such checks are undertaken at set periods and that this forms a specific part of someone's role. A record should be signed to show that this has been done.

As discussed previously, barrier tape and evidence bags can be useful in the worst-case scenarios, but day to day, access to temporary queue management cordons can allow flexible control of an area and access. It is also important that the exit points and places of safety are considered should staff need to withdraw during an incident. Where secure areas are established it is important that they contain a telephone to summon assistance. The scenario of a staff member or other person being taken hostage also needs to be considered.

Sanctions

8.12 Many airlines and hospital trusts operate warning systems, for example they issue a letter to a disruptive individual or a red warning card. Clear sanctions play an important part in preventing and responding to violent behaviour. However it must be recognised that confronting individual/s in this manner could be the trigger of an assault. It is essential that staff are taught how to accurately assess people and situations and are provided with training in when, where and how to confront a violent person. Some organisations are quick to launch these schemes but do not consider the position of the manager or member of staff who has to carry out these difficult and high risk tasks.

Training

8.13 Training will focus firstly on raising safety awareness and reducing risk. This is largely knowledge-based and staff also need to develop the skills, attitudes and behaviours for dealing with the incident that does occur. These skills are explored extensively in CHAPTER 7 TRAINING. If staff are to develop confidence in managing violence the training will need to be dynamic and realistic, and cover the key scenarios identified.

Teamwork will be tested during stressful incidents and this should also be a key consideration in staff development to ensure staff communicate effectively, understand their responsibilities and respect each other. This should also extend to the wider team operating in a certain area, as communication often breaks down across a role or function.

Physical fitness is particularly important and vital in some roles where staff are expected to respond to violence. Looking and feeling fit and behaving professionally will help to earn respect and deter assault. Fitness will also play a vital part when restraining a violent person or even running away from one.

Rehearsal and testing

8.14   Without doubt rehearsal and testing is one of the most under-rated and least performed aspects of incident management. With the exception of some areas of the emergency services, psychiatric care and the armed forces, organisations rarely practice their response to violent incidents. This is somewhat strange as for example most organisations have regular fire drills to test communications and procedures.

In sport, coaches are often heard telling athletes 'you play as you train' and the same principle applies to incident management. Realistic practice and scenario-based training will make a big difference to the effectiveness of the incident response. Unforeseen problems with communications, equipment and procedures will be highlighted through a rehearsal and staff can be actively involved in solving these.

In some areas of work it will be beneficial to set up multi-agency exercises involving the police and other agencies. This helps to clarify expectations and iron out any problems.

Review and improvement

8.15   Review and improvement come from two sources. Firstly, the training, testing and rehearsing of processes and procedures will provide important information about their effectiveness. It is important to seek the views, opinions and reactions of the people who have taken part and this is done most effectively be reviewing the experience as a whole team, using the Learning Review Model which is shown in CHAPTER 9. The more realistic the situations used, the more effective the feedback.

The second source is the detailed examination of real incidents. This is covered in CHAPTER 9 from the perspective of the people who have been involved and they all need a thorough review to ensure that the individuals concerned and the organisation learn from it. It is also important to sensitively examine how the incident was managed and how effective, or otherwise, the plans, practices and procedures were when tested in the real situation.

Checklist

8.16

❑	Assess the risk – does your organisation face a foreseeable risk of serious incidents of violence towards staff?
❑	Are roles, responsibilities and communication lines clearly identified for the management of an incident of workplace violence?
❑	Are the individuals and departments concerned aware of the roles, responsibilities and communication lines?
❑	Is the risk to staff and other service users great enough to warrant the development of specially trained response teams?
❑	Are the leadership roles and decision-making levels clear and have the appropriate people received training for taking a lead role in such incidents?
❑	Are there clear procedures outlined for managing the different aspects of an incident? In particular, for serious incidents are there clear procedures for securing and preserving evidence?
❑	Is there a clear strategy for managing communications and the media in the event of an incident?
❑	Has specialist equipment been identified and have staff been trained in its use in the event of an incident?
❑	Have the all the people who might be called upon to respond to an incident received appropriate training?
❑	Is there a robust and regular method in place for rehearsing and testing the complete response to an incident?
❑	Is there a review and evaluation process in place to provide feedback about the effectiveness of the incident management either after a test or a real incident?

9 Post-incident Management

Introduction

9.1 The consequences of being a victim of workplace violence can be far reaching. In the worst case it can result in a complete loss of confidence, loss of job and, perhaps having to learn to live with a disabling physical or mental injury. Monetary compensation, though welcome, rarely compensates for the physical and mental scars that can be left following the trauma of being subjected to violence.

Employers are increasingly paying substantial settlements to employees who have experienced stress-related illness as the result of traumatic incidents, or continuous low-level abuse over a period of time. Organisations that do not take adequate steps to prevent such incidents or fail to respond appropriately when they occur are vulnerable to both civil and criminal litigation, with personal liability to managers and executives.

The importance of a policy, competent risk assessment and effective risk reduction measures have been highlighted throughout this handbook as vital elements in minimising the possibility of a member of staff being subjected to violence. Sadly, this is not the end of the story and it is clear that even the most comprehensive measures cannot completely prevent incidents of workplace violence from taking place. It is important, therefore, to complete the circle and ensure that the aftermath of workplace violence is given as much attention as the other elements that make up a comprehensive approach to dealing with this issue.

This chapter will explore the ways that people react to being victims of violence and aggression. It will then go on to examine the ways that an organisation can provide support and help for staff who are involved.

Traditionally post-incident support in large organisations has been the domain of welfare or occupational health departments. However this chapter shifts the primary focus to line management. In many smaller organisations it is not viable to have dedicated support services, and even where they exist they can be far removed from operational staff. Although it is important to offer confidential support lines and occupational health support, these form one part of the solution as victims of violence often fail to recognise that they need help, or are reluctant to ask for it. It is the sensitive and practical support of managers and colleagues that so often makes the difference for victims, and where further help is needed it is often these groups that facilitate it. This is why education at all levels is important, and should be supported by a clear policy and procedure, and specialist support when needed.

Many victims are often confused or afraid of the legal process that may take place after an assault – this chapter will follow a typical case through the criminal justice system. Finally, the chapter will look at the important issue of learning from the incidents and explore ways in which the organisation and individual can develop as a result.

How people are affected by workplace violence

9.2   Perhaps the most important thing to recognise is that everyone has a different way of responding to and dealing with the aftermath of a violent or aggressive incident. There is no right or wrong way to react and people must be allowed to deal with it in their own way.

Being the victim of violence is particularly traumatic because it involves an interaction with another person at a very personal level and this can produce some difficult and complex emotional reactions.

Having said that, it is possible to categorise a range of typical reactions that may follow when someone has become the victim of an incident. They fall into three time periods and understanding these different reactions is helpful when supporting someone through the different stages of recovering from the incident.

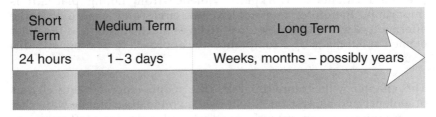

Short Term	Medium Term	Long Term
24 hours	1–3 days	Weeks, months – possibly years

Figure 9.1: Timescale of reactions to workplace violence

Short-term reactions

9.3   In the first few hours following the incident, the victim will have some initial reactions to the aggression and violence directed at them. These reactions are predominantly emotional and are a direct response to the incident. Many factors will influence the severity of the reaction, not least of which is the individual's level of resilience towards traumatic situations.

The level of aggression, suddenness of the confrontation and physical injury sustained are also some of the factors which will influence how the victim will react. The following are the most likely reactions to result:

- Shock, confusion, disbelief, fear, helplessness

  It is quite common for a victim to find it hard to believe that it happened at all. They are likely to be in a state of shock and may cry, shake and feel physically sick. They may also be in physical pain as a result of an assault.

- Anger, embarrassment, feeling of violation

  Anger towards the perpetrator is a natural reaction and the victim might swear, shout or behave aggressively either towards the offender if he or she is still around, or it may displaced towards other people. The victim may feel embarrassed about what happened and may have feelings of having been violated both physically and emotionally by the aggressor.

Many of these initial reactions will begin to lessen as the victim moves into the next phase.

Medium-term reactions

9.4   The short-term reactions are characterised by their 'immediate' nature, formed before the victim has had any time to think about, and begun to rationalise, what has happened. The medium-term reactions begin to appear when the victim has had a chance to consider the incident, to work though what happened and to think about the consequences, near misses and alternatives. This will be around 24-hours after the incident. Reactions can include:

- Feelings of loss, guilt, shame, embarrassment, humiliation

  Many victims start to blame themselves for what happened. The 'what if' questions start to surface and they see lots of ways the incident could have been avoided – leading to guilt and embarrassment that they were unable to prevent it. A feeling of loss of control can be quite acute. The victim's world has changed because they were unable to prevent another person from harming them.

- Exhaustion and tiredness, lack of sleep

  It is quite natural to experience great tiredness and exhaustion after a traumatic and difficult incident. The body's 'flight or fight' reaction has dumped a cocktail of chemicals into the victim's system to help him or her cope and, as these wear off, the body needs time to rest and recuperate. This can be made worse because the victim finds it hard sleep – often because he or she is continuously thinking about the incident. Victims may experience 'flashbacks' which are in effect a re-living of the event and all the feelings and senses associated with it.

- Denial of effects, ready to get back to work

  Equally common is a denial of any effects. The victim claims to be fine and is keen to get back to work and put it all behind him or her. This may well be the case, of course, as some people do have the ability to deal with such incidents very positively. On the other hand, it may well be a 'coping strategy' aimed at being busy so that they don't have to think about it. Victims sometimes become withdrawn, believing that others who were not involved would not understand how they felt, and as a result are reluctant to share their feelings or ask for assistance.

- Anger, frustration and resentment

  The victim may well begin to feel anger towards other people who were involved in the incident and towards the organisation – this may be in the form of anger towards managers, because they did not do enough to prevent it.

- Lack of confidence, anxiety about similar situations or meeting the aggressor

  The victim's work environment has changed in that he or she may now feel much more vulnerable than before the incident. They may be particularly worried about finding themselves in a similar situation. They may also have fears about being approached or harassed by the offender. There is a risk that they may over react or respond inappropriately, in other situations in which they feel threatened.

Moving successfully through this medium-term phase is often the key to recovery. Once the victim has acknowledged what has happened and come to terms with it then he or she can then move back towards a normal life. Line managers can provide vital support in this phase and are pivotal in the successful recovery of most of the victims. This will be considered in more detail later in the chapter.

Long-term reactions

9.5   Generally, reactions that persist beyond a couple of weeks of the incident are indicative that the victim is finding difficulty in coming to terms with the incident and that he or she probably needs professional specialist help. Examples include:

- Persistent tiredness, exhaustion, depression, bouts of anxiety

  Sometimes the victim seems unable to 'pick himself up' after the incident and will display changed behaviour for a sustained period of time. He or she may take a lot of short periods of sick leave or go on long-term sick leave.

- Excessive drinking and smoking, anti-social behaviour, irritable and aggressive behaviour

Many of these reactions will be most evident in the victim's home or social environments although they may appear well during work.

• Nightmares, flashbacks, headaches, nausea, difficulty in eating and sleeping

These are common physical reactions that manifest themselves in victims who continue to be traumatised by the incident.

A victim who displays these long-term reactions clearly needs specialised help, and an organisation which wants to provide a complete response to the range of issues that result from workplace violence, will be set up facilities to deal with this.

Recovering from the incident

9.6   The turning point for most victims is the acceptance of what has happened to them. Once they accept the incident as a reality, they stop going through the 'if only' scenarios and stop blaming themselves for what took place.

There are many factors that will determine how quickly a person will recover from such an event and it is almost impossible to predict the course of an individual's return to a normal life. Simplistic connections between, for example, being 'male, and physically strong' and 'recovering more quickly' do not necessarily work. A 'macho' man who is proud of his physical abilities can quickly be undermined if he is assaulted by someone who is apparently weaker then he is. His world has been changed by the incident and he may find it harder to cope with recovery. This can be made more difficult if the victim is in an organisation with a 'macho' culture (where it would be seen as a weakness); a culture where it is difficult to approach management; or one where violence is accepted as part of the job – as it has commonly been viewed in care and security roles.

It is difficult to guess what might be going on in someone else's life and there are many things that could have an effect on recovery. These might include the person's family background, the level of stress already existing in his or her life, the existence of a previous similar encounter or event and the existence, or otherwise, of a partner or network of family and friends. These factors are important and need to be borne in mind by people in the organisation who have a responsibility to help and support victims of workplace violence.

Returning to normal

9.7   Most people reach a point where they can move on from the event and get back to their normal daily lives. They achieve this when they regain confidence and self esteem and recognise that, although life has changed in some aspects as a result of what occurred, they can become positive about being back in their working environment.

Although these various reactions have been described in discrete stages it will be rare for anyone to pass smoothly through them all. In reality, many things will cause a victim to progress and regress in the move towards normality. The return to work, for example, can be quite difficult and bring back feelings of insecurity and fear. Having to appear in court as a witness or learning of a colleague who has been involved in a similar incident may well trigger a reoccurrence of one or more of the reactions previously experienced.

For a few people, a return to 'normal' is virtually impossible, particularly if they have been permanently disabled by physical or mental injury. In such cases, the victim will need the most specialised care and support in trying to come to terms with their circumstances.

Thankfully, for most people the support of family, friends, colleagues and managers will be enough to help them recover from the trauma of the incident and return to a normal working life.

Providing post-incident support

9.8   An appropriate post-incident support system should be an integral part of an organisation's overall response to workplace violence. The sophistication of the support system will depend upon the level of risk to which the staff are being exposed.

Staff working in the emergency services can often experience violent and other traumatic events, and therefore require a high level of post-incident support. This will range from line manager support, formal de-briefing processes, to occupational health services, which will include access to specialist help for the most serious consequences of work-related violence. Some organisations adopt formal psychological de-briefing processes, sometimes referred to as Critical Incident Stress De-briefing. Although these approaches have considerable support in some areas, there is ongoing debate about their value, and concern at the potential risks associated with victims 're-living' the traumatic experience in the de-briefing process. Whether or not the organisation adopts a formal de-briefing process, it is essential that support mechanisms and procedures are put in place for managers and staff.

Even where the frequency of serious incidents is low, the organisation should have a post-incident support procedure and line managers should be trained in the skills appropriate to helping a victim through the first stages of coping with an incident of work-related violence. It should also be possible to access specialist help if necessary.

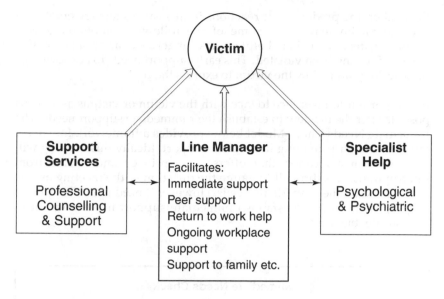

Figure 9.2: Supporting the victim

The role of the line manager

9.9   In the vast majority of cases the support for the victim will be provided through his or her line manager. The short and medium-term reactions following an incident have been described in **9.3** and **9.4** and the focus of the line manager's support will be concentrated on helping the victim work though those reactions and in facilitating further support where necessary. Successfully dealing with these phases is vital in providing the optimum conditions for the individual to recover and return to a normal working life.

There are three points at which this support is crucial:

- Immediately after the incident has happened.

- During any absence from work.

- Preparing for and returning to work.

Immediately after the incident has happened

9.10   The first consideration should be for the health of the victim. If they need medical treatment then this should take priority over any other considerations. Evidential issues also need to be considered (see CHAPTER 8 INCIDENT MANAGEMENT).

Remember, the predominant reactions in this early stage are emotional and the victim may show some of the following emotions; shock, confusion, fear, disbelief, helplessness, anger, embarrassment and a feeling of having been violated. This early support needs to acknowledge those feelings and allow the victim to express them.

It is important to meet face to face with the victim or victims as soon as possible after the incident to establish their immediate support needs. The Immediate Needs Check Model below provides a framework for such a meeting and for providing immediate support. Ideally this meeting will take place in a location that offers some privacy and is free from interruptions. It is difficult to gauge the duration of the meeting as this will depend on the individuals needs. However it need not be lengthy as its purpose is solely to establish immediate support needs and not to 'investigate' the incident.

Immediate Needs Check				
Stage One Introduction	**Stage Two** Listen to the victim's account	**Stage Three** What does the victim need?	**Stage Four** Provide Information	**Stage Five** Conclusion – next meeting

Figure 9.3: Immediate needs check

Stage One – introduction

9.11

- The physical well-being of the victim is the prime consideration and it should be established if the victim has any physical injuries which need attention.

- It is important that the victim understands the nature and extent of the meeting and it should be emphasised that its purpose is to provide support, information and meet the immediate needs of the victim.

- The direct line manager may be perceived as an authority figure and it should be recognised that the victim may see it this way. An alternative should be offered if there appears to be any conflict. If the immediate line manager is not in a position to meet the victim following the incident, then a mechanism needs to be in place to ensure another appropriate person does so.

Stage Two – listen to the victim

9.12

- Part of the process of dealing with the emotions and feelings related to such an incident is for the victim to be able to relate what has happened to him or her. The line manager should actively listen, acknowledging the victim's feelings but without judging or offering an opinion. If the victim does not wish to talk about the incident they should not be pressured to, as this can happen at a later stage when learning can also be drawn from the incident. The police may however need to speak to the victim and witnesses sooner, particularly if a major crime has taken place.

Stage Three – what does the victim need?

9.13

- The victim will no doubt have some immediate needs following the incident. They may for example wish to make telephone calls, contact family or friends or make arrangements to get home.

- Minimising the immediate problems and anxieties of the victim will make it easier for him or her to deal with the emotions and reactions to the incident itself. Help may be given to them by for example reducing or removing their workload.

Stage 4 – providing information

9.14

- It helps the victim to realise that the reactions that he or she is experiencing are quite normal and to be expected. It may help to outline some of the reactions that might be felt as time progresses.

- The victim needs to be aware of counselling, after care services and specialist help that is available through the organisation and how to access them.

Stage 5 – conclusion and next meeting

9.15

- A final check on the immediate welfare needs of the victim is needed and practical arrangements should be made for getting them home etc.

- Many victims complain that although they are treated very well straight after the incident, they often see nobody during the days following the incident. It is important to make a firm arrangement to see the victim again with the next few days.

Other immediate post-incident considerations

9.16   There will be a need to complete the workplace violence report form, which will require a formal narrative of the incident. For evidential reasons, this should wherever possible be completed personally by the victim as soon as practicable after the incident. Every effort should be made to get the victim to complete at least the basic requirements whilst it is fresh in his or her memory.

It is tempting to leave this task but it can have far reaching consequences if the incident becomes the subject of criminal or civil proceedings. An accurate and early account of the incident can make all the difference to the outcome of a case. This may not always be possible if the victim is severely injured or traumatised.

During any absence from work

9.17   It is easy to lose contact with people when they are away from work, and it is vital to plan visits and communications. Whilst colleagues may be consumed by work tasks, victims of violence may be at home constantly thinking about what happened. Line managers should co-ordinate contact by colleagues whilst the individual is absent. The nature and extent of the contact will depend on the desires of the individual, but options include, personal visits, telephone contact and gifts.

If managers feel that too much contact on their part may not be welcome they can encourage visits by close colleagues and friends. A key friend or colleague could become the key link in cases where a person is absent for longer periods. Remember also that the victim's family members may also be finding it hard to cope and they too will probably appreciate offers of help and being asked about their well being.

Preparing for and returning to work

9.18   The victim's return to work may take place quickly and with little apparent difficulty. On the other hand, he or she may have a period of time off work to recover from the physical and/ or mental effects of the incident.

Once again, the line manager is pivotal in the success or otherwise of the return to work. Remember the complex emotions, feelings and reactions that might be affecting the victim at this point eg:

- Feelings of loss, guilt, shame, embarrassment, humiliation.

- Exhaustion and tiredness, lack of sleep.

- Denial of effects, readiness to get back to work.

196

- Anger, frustration and resentment.

- Lack of confidence, anxiety about similar situations or meeting the aggressor.

Managing the victim's return to work must take into account the possibility that one or more of these reactions will be experienced by the victim. It is important not to over react and become too protective but equally important is the need to deal with any issues sensitively and supportively. The following is offered as a framework for managing the back to work process.

Pre-return contact

9.19   It is helpful to contact the victim before they return to work, preferably in person. The line manager should discuss the practical aspects of returning to work and establish what he or she needs in terms of support and help. This will then form the basis of the process.

Return to work

9.20   Some people will want to return to work with the minimum of fuss. Other people might want more help. These different needs should be respected and managers and colleagues need to avoid being over protective towards the victim. If the person has expressed some anxiety or doubts about his or her ability to cope then a range of options can be considered:

- Working in company with a colleague

  This can be very helpful in boosting confidence and allowing the person to do their job but have the support of someone else until his or her confidence remains.

- Minimising contact with clients etc

  Many roles have duties connected with them where the contact with the client, service user or public is minimised or less confrontational. A spell on these 'lighter' duties may help to regain confidence.

- Spending time with the victim

  As a line manager, spending more time with the victim in the first few days after his or her return to work may help the victim to talk about the incident and aftermath. It is common for the victim to resent the organisation and management for what happened, and to feel that they could have done more. Such concerns need to be listened to and actively pursued.

- 'Short-term' working

  This may be particularly appropriate after a long period of sick leave where the victim returns to work for a few hours a day to help the reintegration into his or her work environment. This can also be a way of alternating the lighter duties with spells back on the individual's 'front line' role.

The first few weeks

9.21   In most cases, the return to work will be completed successfully and the victim will quickly return to his or her normal working. The line manager needs to keep an eye on the individual's behaviour as the weeks progress – particularly where he or she is working in circumstances similar to those in which the incident occurred. A victim may, for example, avoid duties or circumstances that make him or her feel vulnerable and which mirror the environment in which he or she was abused, attacked or threatened. For example a conductor may not pursue fares, or may avoid checking tickets at night. This can be subtle and the victim may not consciously be aware of such behaviour but they may need extra support in such circumstances. It is also possible that the individual will become hyper, vigilant and over react in situations. This will impact on colleagues who may become protective, and increase risk to everyone.

The line manager should have an informal review with the individual a few weeks after the return to work to ensure that he or she feels recovered from the incident and that he or she has received all the support and help needed.

Avoiding blame

9.22   The issue of blame in relation to workplace violence needs a special mention. Incidents of workplace violence take place in the context of a conflict with a client, service user or other member of the public. Such encounters can become heated, emotional and unpredictable and the member of staff is often doing their best to resolve the situation in very trying circumstances. Very few people are minded to invite abuse, threats or assault upon themselves and most are trying to deal with the conflict in a way that avoids violence and aggression.

In the subsequent investigation of what happened, the 'heat' of the encounter and the practical difficulties involved are hard to imagine. The investigator is also gifted with the benefit of hindsight and it is easy to see what went wrong, how it should have been handled and which policies or practices were not followed. This can all too easily end with a statement that suggests: ' … had the member of staff followed the company policy then this assault would not have happened'.

If an organisation takes the issue of workplace violence seriously, then it must recognise that nothing gives the right to a service user or member of the public to abuse, threaten or assault a member of their staff. If it happens, the member of staff is the victim – and the victim should not be blamed for what happened to them.

This is not to say that staff do not make mistakes in the way that they handle these incidents. Indeed, it would be hard not to make mistakes in the unpredictable and difficult circumstances that often surround incidents of workplace violence and, of course, it is important that both the individual and the organisation should learn from the way things were handled. The point is that the victim should not feel blamed for the actions of the offender.

Some employees may experience more violence than others and one of the reasons for this may be their attitude or behaviour. Effective management systems can identify such trends and any personal development needs.

The last part of this chapter will look at ways of learning from the incident.

Line manager training needs

9.23   The importance of training the line managers in the management of workplace violence cannot be over emphasised as they play a vital role in almost every aspect of the organisational response to the issue. This includes involvement in the development and implementation of policy, the process of reporting, recording and monitoring incidents and support for the victims.

Providing support requires the development of special skills. Whilst line managers should not be expected to be skilled in counselling, they do need to develop their ability to communicate, listen actively, empathise and provide appropriate levels of support for the people who they are responsible for. They need to understand the issues and be aware of the range of help available to victims and how to access it. They need to be able to recognise the signs and symptoms of stress and the different reactions that might be encountered, together with an understanding of the appropriate responses to each.

In short, the training needs for line managers involved in the management of workplace violence are varied and complex and there is an obligation on the organisation to ensure that these training needs are met.

Support services

9.24   There is a point where some victims need more help than the line manager can be expected to offer. If an individual is suffering from the sort of persistent reactions already discussed in the medium to long term following the incident then they should be referred to more professional help. In this context it will probably consist of professional counselling.

Larger organisations will probably have an occupational health department, which will be geared up to provide the sort of help required. Smaller organisations can 'buy in' counselling services on an ad hoc basis. There may be a temptation to train internal people in counselling skills to provide an in-house team of counsellors. This may be a good idea in principle but there are important issues of both credibility and confidentiality to think about.

Occasionally, a victim may find it impossible to move on from the incident. Some may develop a condition called post-traumatic stress disorder or exhibit some of the symptoms of it. In all these cases, the victim will need specialist psychological and psychiatric help. Remember the reactions outlined earlier that may indicate that an individual is in need of specialist help. Sometimes colleagues will bring attention to the fact that the individual is simply not 'his normal self'.

Preparing for the worst

9.25 Organisations need to be in a position to quickly access expert management advice following incidents that are likely to have a severe impact on individuals and / or the organisation. It is important to plan this in advance as poor quality decisions can easily be made when emotions are high and everyone is under pressure. Plans should include access to advice and support concerning:

- Professional help for employees, service users, families and partners.
- Advice on legal issues.
- Advice on managing media attention.

Victim Support

9.26 Victim Support is a national organisation with a great deal of experience in helping people to cope with being the victim of a crime, regardless of whether it has been reported to the police.

It provides confidential, practical and emotional support through a network of local schemes across England, Wales and Northern Ireland. A sister organisation exists for Scotland (telephone: 0131 662 4486) and the Republic of Ireland (telephone: (00) 353 1878 0870).

The victim support line (telephone: 0845 30 30 900) is open 9 am to 9 pm weekdays, 9 am to 7 pm weekends, and 9 am to 9 pm on Bank Holidays.

The support line exists to enable any one concerned about crime to talk to a trained helper.

They also produce a helpful handbook *Helping People Cope with Crime* (ISBN 0 340 78049 5).

Victim Support also runs the Witness Support Service (referred to later in **9.31**).

The police investigation and court case

9.27   Most victims want to see their aggressor brought to justice. However, it may prove to be quite a daunting process and it can help to be aware of how the process works and what they might expect. There are several prosecution routes including:

- Prosecution through the police to the Crown Prosecution Service, or, in Scotland, the Crown Office and Procurator Fiscal Service (see **9.28**).

- Private prosecution (a similar process as above but instigated through a solicitor and not the police. This is rare in Scotland.)

- Civil prosecution (instigated through a solicitor in a civil court).

Prosecution through the police is the most common route. However employers should have a clear policy and guidance on other avenues available should the police or Crown Prosecution Service decide not to progress a matter. This should include the degree of support they can provide, such as funding and time off for the legal process in preparing and giving evidence. South West Trains Ltd is explicit in this regard in its 'Personal Safety Handbook':

'If the CPS decides not to prosecute, you may still be able to do so with South West Trains' help. If you wish to pursue the matter you or your manager can contact the company's claims manager. After hearing all the facts he will consult with a solicitor and decide whether there is sufficient evidence for you to bring a successful private prosecution. If there is, the company will fund the prosecution, which will be in your name, retaining a barrister to appear in court for you'.

Trade unions have also funded legal action by members and the 'No win, No fee' approaches are increasingly being offered by law firms. Unfortunately many lawyers currently have limited knowledge and experience concerning the effective management of violence and related issues such as the use of force. This can result in their applying for criminal injuries compensation, when in fact there could have been a strong case for a prosecution. This will change as victims, law firms, insurance companies, and unions become more aware of the potential for successful prosecutions on work-related violence issues, and as case law develops. It is unfortunate that such action is needed to motivate some employers to address and resource this issue properly.

Criminal and civil courts provide further protection from harassment and violence in a number of ways, including:

- Injunctions.

- Restraining orders (eg preventing convicted persons contacting the victim/s).

- Anti-social Behaviour Orders.

When a court order is in place, the police are in a strong position to take action should it be breached.

Note: Offences can carry extra penalties if proven to be racially aggravated, and constitute a more serious offence under the *Crime and Disorder Act 1998*. Further information on legislation can be found in CHAPTER 2.

As can be seen from figure 9.4 (below), the process falls into three main phases:

1. The police investigation.

2. The Crown Prosecution Service or Crown Office and Procurator Fiscal Service.

3. The court case.

The police investigation

9.28   A typical incident of workplace violence might end in the victim being punched in the face by the offender causing a split lip and severe bruising to the eyes and face. The sequence of events that follow will begin with a report to the police.

- A police officer will interview the victim and take a detailed statement about all the circumstances surrounding the incident, including a description of the offender. The officer will also require details of all the witnesses to the incident so that statements may also be obtained from them.

- In a case involving a physical injury, the victim may be medically examined to establish the extent of the injuries. Any forensic evidence may be taken (any fibres or material transferred from the offender) and the injuries may be photographed to provide evidence for court.

- In this type of case it is quite probable that the victim will be asked to formally identify the offender if he or she is located. This can be done in a variety of ways and might involve looking at photos or a video of a series of people, identifying the offender in a location

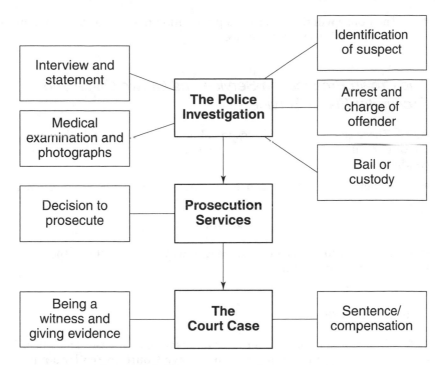

Figure 9.4: The process of a prosecution

such as a street or shopping precinct or through a formal identification parade (behind one-way glass).

- When enough evidence has been gathered, the suspect may be arrested and interviewed and dependant on the standard of evidence may then be charged with an offence. In certain circumstances, outlined in national guidelines, the offender will be cautioned for the offence. This would be unlikely in the type of case under consideration.

- Once charged, the police must release the offender on bail unless there are special reasons why they think he or she should not be released. These might include the seriousness of the crime or fears that he or she will interfere with witnesses. If this is the case, the offender will be kept in custody and taken before a court where the issues will be considered. If he or she is released on bail the court can impose conditions that can include:

  o regular reporting to the police;

  o residency restrictions;

  o keeping away from specified locations;

  o having no contact with specified persons.

- The police will then prepare a prosecution file, for consideration by the Crown Prosecution Service.

The Crown Prosecution Service and Crown Office and Procurator Fiscal Service

9.29 These services have the responsibility for deciding whether or not the case should go forward to court. They make the decision based on two conditions:

- Is there sufficient evidence to provide a realistic prospect of a conviction?

- Is the prosecution in the public interest?

If the decision is to prosecute then the case will go ahead. If not, the police will inform the victim of the decision.

The court case

9.30 Depending upon a variety of circumstances, the case can be heard either in a magistrates' court or at the Crown Court. In Scotland minor cases are heard in the district court or Sheriff Summary Court, and more serious cases are tried by jury in the Sheriff Solemn or High Court of Justiciary.

- If the offender pleads guilty there will be no need for the witnesses to attend court. A summary of the case will be presented, the offenders antecedent history, including any criminal record, will be given to the court. Sentence will be passed and the police will inform the victim of the outcome. Adult courts are open to the public and anyone can go along to observe the proceedings.

- If the offender pleads not guilty then a trial will take place and the witnesses will be warned to attend court to give evidence.

- The proceedings in both the magistrates' court and Crown Court are very similar. The biggest difference is that the Crown Court has a jury who will decide whether the offender is guilty whereas the magistrates will decide in the lower court. The Crown Court is a much more formal and imposing place and giving evidence there is more intimidating.

- A witness will not be allowed to view the proceedings until he or she has given evidence. When called to give evidence, the prosecution solicitor or barrister will take the witness through his or her evidence – basing it upon the original statement made to the police. The defence solicitor or barrister will then cross examine the witness about the evidence he or she has given. Finally, the prosecution will re-examine the witness to clarify and reinforce any points. The judge or magistrate may also ask questions of the witness.

- At the conclusion of all the evidence, the prosecution and defence will sum up their cases and the magistrates will consider the evidence. In the Crown Court, the judge will provide a summary of the case and the jury will consider the evidence.

- If the verdict is not guilty, the offender will be free to leave. If the verdict is guilty the magistrates or the judge will pass sentence after hearing about the offenders antecedent history, any criminal record and any social reports.

Support during the process of the investigation and court case

9.31   The preceding discussion has provided a very condensed outline of the progress of a typical case. It can be a very difficult time for anyone who has to undergo this process.

As mentioned earlier, Victim Support is an organisation with many years of experience in helping people to cope with all the different aspects of surviving the trauma of being the victim of a crime. They have developed a Witness Support Service, which will provide practical help and support for anyone who has to attend Crown Court as a witness.

Learning from the incident

9.32   A great deal of learning can be gained from working though the circumstances of an incident of workplace violence. There is a tendency to concentrate on the negative aspects – the things that went wrong – and to forget the many things that were probably done well. The incident reporting and review process should include an examination of the circumstances, and be designed to highlight the things that were done well and the things that might be improved. This will include learning for both the individuals and the organisation.

As outlined earlier, it is important that any learning process is managed carefully to ensure that it does not seek to 'blame' those who have been the victims of violence, as this will affect their recovery. This is one of the reasons why it is important that team leaders and managers are taught how to 'facilitate' any type of operational de-briefing that an organisation adopts, and the 'learning review' process outlined below (**9.33**). Where individuals have been traumatised it may not be appropriate to involve them directly in the learning review process until they are ready for this.

Where police are likely to be involved in a criminal investigation it is also important to seek their advice before holding any de-briefing or learning review process, as they may wish to interview staff and take statements first. In major incidents the police may secure the area and keep staff and witnesses there until this has been done.

It should be remembered that records of any learning review or de-briefing process will be disclosable, and may be required in any subsequent legal action.

The learning review

9.33   Kolb's Experiential Learning Cycle (figure 9.5 below) provides managers with a simple continuous improvement tool that can be used to draw learning from a specific incident on an individual or group basis. It will also be useful more generally, for example, following an operation or exercise, or at team meetings to review and facilitate best practice. This could be done at the end of a shift, or at a weekly or monthly forum.

What happened?

9.34   The first phase is to get the individual or group to describe what happened during the incident, from their perspective. Everybody should have the opportunity to contribute their version of events. This process helps those involved to better understand the part others played and helps to avoid assumptions about why a colleague did or did not do something. It is important that people are discouraged from drawing conclusions at this stage, and also from making judgements about the actions of others. When a general agreement has been reached that all the points have been covered, the process should move to the next stage of the cycle.

Why did it happen?

9.35   The next stage is to examine the reasons why things went the way that they did. This may highlight organisational or team problems, for example concerning issues such as policy, procedures, systems or communications. It is important to establish which things were successful and why, and which things were not successful and why.

What to do next time?

9.36   The final part of the learning review is to identify the learning from the conclusions and find alternative ways of preventing or responding to a similar incident in the future. Some of this will be learning for individuals and some will be helpful to the development of the team. Much can be gained through creating an open and honest learning environment and internal team and organisational conflicts and falls outs between staff can be reduced. The learning review is equally useful for de-briefing a successful project or activity to ensure that the key success factors are identified, shared and replicated in the future.

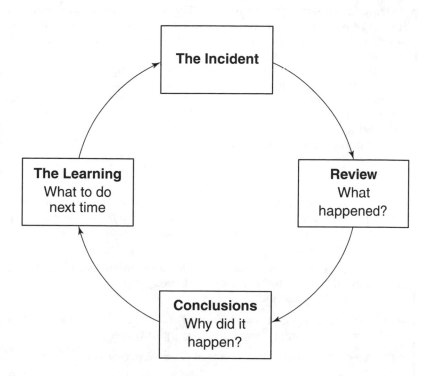

Figure 9.5: The Experiential Learning Cycle

The results of the learning review process should form the basis of a learning action plan for the individuals concerned. Learning for the organisation should to be fed back into the system through the reporting process in the form of recommendations to the workplace violence co-ordinator. It is also important to share key lessons across the wider organisation and possibly with others in the locality or sector. Of course, it is important that both the individual and the organisation should learn from the way things were handled.

Case study – combined internal and external response

9.37

Select Service Partner

Select Service Partner (SSP) has recently trained its bar managers in the how to prevent and respond to violent incidents and in how to provide immediate support to staff. The new initiative also involves the development of regional 'conflict facilitators' who provide additional support to the bar managers and ensure staff in other retail outlets receive training. The conflict facilitators have undergone specialist training that also equips them to follow up violent incidents, to facilitate support for staff involved, and to draw and share any learning. A key tool for the facilitators is a dedicated violence reporting process that provides quality information on incidents and records the follow up process. This reporting process is explored in the context of reporting in CHAPTER 5.

Conclusions

SSP has developed a comprehensive response to violence, and although it is too early to judge its effectiveness it contains key elements that should ensure effective post-incident management including:

- Training locally in post-incident management supported at a regional level by carefully selected and trained managers ('conflict facilitators').

- Clear responsibilities and support at local, regional, and national level, with simple flow charts to support these.

- Access to expert advice through external providers.

- An effective reporting mechanism that underpins training, staff support and management response.

SSP conflict facilitator

9.38 Figure 9.6 (below) shows a flow chart that outlines the SSP conflict facilitator's post-incident response.

Select Service Partner: Conflict Facilitator Responsibilities

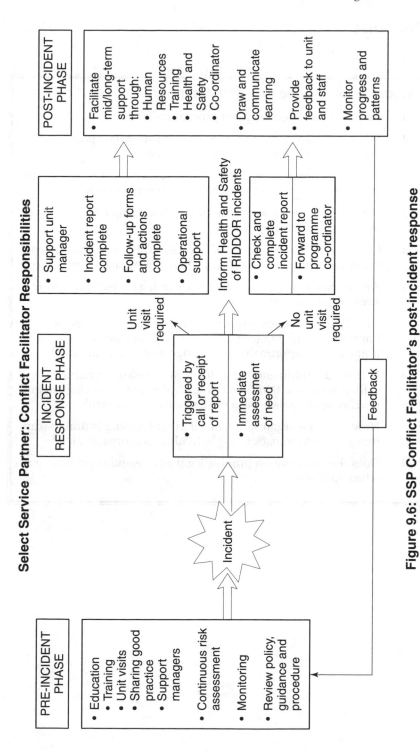

Figure 9.6: SSP Conflict Facilitator's post-incident response

Checklist

9.39

Comprehensive post-incident support

❏   Are there clear post-incident procedures?

❏   What provision is available to provide immediate post-incident support to a victim of workplace violence?

❏   What provision is available to provide support to the victim after the incident and before he or she returns to work?

❏   What provision is available to provide longer-term support following the return to work?

❏   Can line managers and staff access additional professional support, including counselling, where it is appropriate?

❏   Are managers aware of the increase in legal cases surrounding stress and psychiatric injury?

❏   Are line managers equipped to assess and respond to immediate and longer-term staff support needs? Are they trained in the appropriate knowledge, skills and attitudes?

❏   Is there a contingency plan for a 'worst-case scenario'? (eg a skilled response team, access to professional psychiatric and psychological assistance, a media management plan).

❏   How does the organisation ensure that learning is drawn from incidents and fed back to the individual and organisation?

❏   Does the organisation provide legal advice and support to staff when appropriate?

Appendix: Associations, organisations and departments connected with workplace violence

Throughout this handbook, several sources of further information, help, and advice have been mentioned. These have included a number of government bodies, private and public organisations, charitable trusts, trade union and professional bodies.

This appendix will draw together these different sources to provide a comprehensive guide to obtaining specialised help and guidance on the areas that have been explored.

Most of the references are to resources on the internet as almost every organisation that can offer help and advice has an website and it is undoubtedly the most effective way of accessing the vast amount of information available. A search on the internet for 'workplace violence' will produce a lot of hits – particularly internet sites in the United States, which have relevance to the subject area and are of academic interest. However, the aim of this handbook is to provide practical help and therefore the resources identified are predominantly UK-based and cited because they offer directly relevant advice and guidance.

UK online

This website is a general gateway into any information, statistics, research, reports, press releases concerning national and local government issues, initiatives and campaigns. It is very user-friendly and is aimed at providing easy access to information and links to specific websites about every aspect of living and working in the UK.

The website address is: www.ukonline.gov.uk.

British Crime Survey

The most informative source of statistical information is the British Crime Survey which conducts a yearly survey into a broad range of crime-related topics, including workplace violence. It can be accessed on the following website: www.homeoffice.gov.uk/rds/bcs1.html.

The website gives access to all the relevant links, including the following specific workplace violence surveys sponsored by the Health and Safety Executive:

- Tracey Budd 'Violence at work: Findings from the British Crime Survey' (October 1999); and

- Tracey Budd 'Violence at work: New findings from the 2000 British Crime Survey' (July 2001).

Health and Safety Executive (HSE)

The HSE itself is the obvious starting point for any enquiries on health and safety in general, and workplace violence in particular. Its website is very comprehensive and contains lots of informative data and links to more specialised help and advice about issues of policy, risk assessment and reduction. The HSE also provides a range of sector-specific publications, which deal with the specific issues of workplace violence in particular organisations.

HSE Information Services
Caerphilly Business Park
Caerphilly
CF83 3GG
Infoline: 08701 545 500 (open 8.30 am to 5 pm Monday to Friday)
Fax: 02920 859 260
Website: www.hse.gov.uk
Email: hseinformationservices@natbrit.com

The HSE also has information centres in Sheffield, London and Bootle (open from 9 am to 5 pm Monday to Friday) for personal callers who want advice.

Sheffield Information Centre
Health and Safety Executive
Health and Safety Laboratory
Broad Lane
Sheffield
S3 7HQ

London Information Centre
Health and Safety Executive
Rose Court, Ground Floor North
2 Southwark Bridge
London
SE1 9HS

Bootle Information Centre
Health and Safety Executive
Magdalen House
Trinity Road
Bootle
Merseyside
L20 3QZ

Department of Health

The Department of Health website hosts the National Task Force on Violence against Health Care Staff. This forum provides an excellent resource on sector-specific issues but also general help on many of the issues raised throughout this handbook.

Department of Health
Richmond House
79 Whitehall
London
SW1A 2NS
Tel: 0207 210 4850 (lines open from 9 am to 5 pm Monday to Friday)
Minicom: 020 7210 5025
Website: www.doh.gov.uk
Email: dhmail@doh.gsi.gov.uk

Trades Union Congress (TUC)

In 1999 the TUC published 'Violent Times', a key report on preventing and managing violence at work, which highlighted many of the contemporary issues of work-related violence. Its website, TUC Online, has a searchable database of press releases, documents, fact sheets, conference and congress reports, which provides up to date information on various issues.

Many trade unions, such as UNISON and TSSA, have undertaken sector-specific research of their own and provide lots of advice, guidance and information for their members about reducing the risks of work-related violence. The TUC site provides links to union websites in the UK.

TUC
Congress House
Great Russell Street
London
WC1B 3LS
Tel: 020 7636 4030
Website: www.tuc.org.uk

National Health Service (NHS)

The NHS has been at the forefront of many initiatives relating to workplace violence. Perhaps the most widely publicised is the Zero Tolerance Campaign. Its website has a specific area devoted to this campaign and is a mine of useful information about the practical ways that the issue can be approached across the health sector. Much of the information, advice and guidance is transferable across to other sectors.

The website can be accessed at: www.nhs.uk; zero tolerance website: www.nhs.uk/zerotolerance.

Institute of Conflict Management (ICM)

The ICM mission statement is:

> 'To develop, monitor and promote professional standards for the effective prevention and management of aggression and conflict at work and to achieve pre-eminence as the national lead body for the setting of standards and accreditation of conflict management training and related services in all sectors.'

The ICM website is useful for updates and information about standards across the sectors and issues relating to conflict management, conferences, reports, media items and research.

ICM
840 Melton Road
Thurmaston
Leicester
LE4 8BN
Tel: 0116 264 0083
Fax: 0116 264 0141
Website: www.conflictmanagement.org
Email: icm@associationhg.org.uk

Institution of Occupational Safety and Health (IOSH)

IOSH is Europe's leading body for health and safety professionals, with over 25,000 members and an expanding international membership in more than 50 countries. As an independent, not-for-profit organisation and guardian of competence in professional practice, IOSH regulates and steers the profession, maintaining standards and providing impartial, authoritative advice on health and safety issues. IOSH has been awarded a Royal Charter.

The following courses are run as part of the extensive Professional Development Training Programme, to which everyone, who needs the training, is welcome:

- Managing work-related violence (2-day course).

- Negotiating skills and handling conflict (3-day course).

- Stress in perspective: Risk assessment and management (2-day course).

- Stress awareness training: Training for trainers (5-day course).

Institution of Occupational Safety and Health
The Grange
Highfield Drive
Wigston
Leicestershire
LE18 1NN
Tel: general – 0116 257 3100; course bookings – 0116 257 3197
Fax: 0116 257 3101
Website: www.iosh.co.uk
Email: general – enquiries@iosh.co.uk; course bookings –
    zoe.whitehead@iosh.co.uk, or, tracey.banks@iosh.co.uk

British Institute of Learning Disabilities (BILD)

The BILD is an organisation that exists to provide support, information research and resources for anyone who has an interest in learning disabilities. It provides a comprehensive website and has taken an important initiative to develop standards around the use of physical intervention in circumstances involving people with learning disabilities. The BILD website provides a range of information, guides, advice, and codes of practice for anyone working in this particular field.

British Institute of Learning Disabilities
Campion House
Green Street
Kidderminster
Worcestershire
DY10 1JL
Tel: 01562 723 010
Fax: 01562 723 029
Website: www.bild.org.uk
Email: enquiries@bild.org.uk

Employment NTO

The Employment NTO represents anyone with a concern for health and safety in the workplace. It recently completed the National Occupational Standards in Managing Work-related Violence (covered in CHAPTER 3) and has also produced National Occupational Standards in Learning and Development.

Both of these sets of National Occupational Standards can be purchased direct from the Employment NTO via their website or orderline (tel: 0116 251 9727).

Employment NTO
Kimberley House
47 Vaughan Way
Leicester
LE1 4SG
Tel: 0116 251 7979
Fax: 0116 251 1464
Website: www.empnto.co.uk
Email: info@empnto.co.uk

Maybo Limited

Maybo Limited is a leading UK specialist in the management of conflict and violence in the workplace. Its pioneering work is helping hundreds of organisations to manage these issues effectively. The company specialises in working with organisations to tailor a complete solution to cater for their specific needs across the whole area of managing work-related violence. Maybo manages the online resource www.workplaceviolence.co.uk. This website has been developed through partnership between the public, private and voluntary sectors. It is non-profit making and the information is provided free of charge to offer a single focal point for managers and front line staff to share ideas and practical solutions. It also provides access to best practice, research and support.

Maybo Limited
59 Berkeley Court
Oatlands Drive
Weybridge
Surrey
KT13 9HY
Tel: 01932 254160
Fax: 01932 260 015
Websites: www.maybo.com and www.workplaceviolence.co.uk
Email: info@maybo.com

Suzy Lamplugh Trust

The Suzy Lamplugh Trust, a registered charity, is a leading authority and campaigner on personal safety issues. The organisation provides a wealth of information, advice and guidance about all aspects of work-related violence, together with training aids, books, booklets, videos, packs, programmes and personal safety attack alarms.

Suzy Lamplugh Trust
14 East Sheen Avenue
London
SW14
Tel: 020 8392 1839
Fax: 020 8392 1830
Website: www.suzylamplugh.org
Email: trust@suzylamplugh.org

Criminal justice system

CJS Online contains information about the processes involved in criminal proceedings and provides extensive advice and guidance for anyone who becomes involved in this process.

The website address is as follows: www.criminal-justice-system.gov.uk.

Crown Prosecution Service (CPS)

The CPS website provides information about the work of the organisation and in particular provides information about the way decisions about prosecutions are made and the code and guidelines which are followed.

The website can be accessed at: www.cps.gov.uk.

The CPS Correspondence Unit can provide general information on the CPS and advice on who to contact. The Unit cannot give legal advice but may be able to offer practical information.

CPS Correspondence Unit
50 Ludgate Hill
London
EC4M 7EX
Tel: 020 7796 8500 (calls may be recorded)
Email: enquiries@cps.gov.uk

Crown Office and Procurator Fiscal Service

The law in Scotland can be quite different from the rest of the UK. This is also true of the legal system and the Crown Office and Procurator Fiscal Service is the Scottish equivalent to the criminal justice system and the CPS. The Crown Office website contains information about the services it offers and advice and guidance about issues like being a witness, as well as links to other useful websites about civil and criminal justice in Scotland.

The website address is: www.crownoffice.gov.uk.

Victim Support

Victim Support is an independent charity which helps people cope with the effects of crime. It provides free and confidential support and information to help people deal with their experience. Its website provides a gateway into the three different sites covering:

- England and Wales and Northern Ireland,

- Scotland, and

- Republic of Ireland.

Essentially it is a very comprehensive 'one stop shop' for information, advice and guidance for the support of victims and witnesses who have been involved in crime.

Victim Support England, Wales and Northern Ireland
National Office
Cranmer House
39 Brixton Road
London
SW9 6DZ
Tel: 020 7735 9166
Fax: 020 7582 5712
Website: www.victimsupport.com
Email: contact@victimsupport.org.uk

Victim Support Scotland
15/23 Hardwell Close
Edinburgh
EH8 9RX
Tel: 0131 668 4486
Fax: 0131 662 5400
Email: info@victimsupportsco.demon.co.uk

Victim Support Ireland
Haliday House
32 Arran Quay
Dublin 7
Tel: 01 8780 870
Fax: 01 8780 944
Email: info@victimsupport.ie

Criminal Injuries Compensation Authority (CICA)

The CICA website is designed to provide information, advice and guidance about the Criminal Injuries Compensation Scheme and to help potential applicants apply for compensation and complete a personal injury or fatal injury application form. (Note: The Criminal Injuries Compensation Board (CICB) ceased to exist after 31 March 2000 when all applicants under consideration transferred to the CICA.)

There are two offices:

CICA
Tay House
300 Bath Street
Glasgow
G2 4LN
Tel: 0141 331 2726
Fax: 0141 331 2287
Website: www.cica.gov.uk
Email: enquiries.cica@gtnet.gov.uk

CICA
Morley House
26–30 Holborn Viaduct
London
EC1A 2JQ
Tel: 020 7842 6800
Fax: 020 7436 0804
Email: enquiries.cica@gtnet.gov.uk

Northern Ireland has it's own scheme:

The Compensation Agency
Royston House
34 Upper Queen Street
Belfast
BT1 6FD
Tel: 028 90 249 944
Website: www.compensationni.gov.uk

Table of Cases

Table of Statutes

Table of Statutory Instruments

Index